Better Homes and Gardens®

Low-Fat & Luscious

Breakfast • Snacks • Main Dishes • Side Dishes • Desserts

BETTER HOMES AND GARDENS® BOOKS
Des Moines, Iowa

BETTER HOMES AND GARDENS® BOOKS
An Imprint of Meredith® Books

Low-Fat & Luscious
Editor: Kristi Fuller, R.D.
Copy Chief: Gregory H. Kayko
Associate Art Director: Lynda Haupert
Recipe Development: Marcia K. Stanley, M.S., R.D.
Contributing Writer: Janet Lepke, R.D.
Electronic Production Coordinator: Paula Forest
Test Kitchen Product Supervisor: Marilyn Cornelius
Food Stylists: Lynn Blanchard, Janet Pittman, Jennifer Peterson
Photographers: Mike Dieter, Scott Little
Contributing Photographer: Kathy Sanders
Production Manager: Douglas Johnston

Director, New Product Development: Ray Wolf
Managing Editor: Christopher Cavanaugh
Test Kitchen Director: Sharon Stilwell

Meredith Publishing Group
President, Publishing Group: Christopher Little
Vice President and Publishing Director: John P. Loughlin

Meredith Corporation
Chairman of the Board and Chief Executive Officer: Jack D. Rehm
President and Chief Operating Officer: William T. Kerr

Chairman of the Executive Committee: E. T. Meredith III

On the front cover: Pasta with Fresh Tomato-Herb Sauce
   (see recipe, page 108)
Photo at right: Blueberry Coffee Cake (see recipe, page 15)

All of us at Better Homes and Gardens® Books are dedicated to providing you with the information and ideas you need to create delicious foods. We welcome your comments and suggestions. Write to us at: Better Homes and Gardens® Books, Cookbook Editorial Department, RW-240, 1716 Locust St., Des Moines, IA 50309-3023

If you would like to order additional copies of any of our books, call 1-800-678-2803 or check with your local bookstore.

Our seal assures you that every recipe in *Low-Fat & Luscious* has been tested in the Better Homes and Gardens® Test Kitchen. This means that each recipe is practical and reliable, and meets our high standards of taste appeal. We guarantee your satisfaction with this book for as long as you own it.

First Edition. Printing Number and Year: 5 4   00 99 98 97
Library of Congress Catalog Card Number: 95-81719
ISBN: 0-696-20373-1

Contents

You'll find all of your traditional breakfast favorites here. French toast, cereal, pancakes, coffeecake—any choice will jump-start your morning in a healthful way.

Next time you have a snack attack or need a party idea, turn to these nutritious and tasty recipes. Remember, snacks and party foods are OK when prepared the low-fat way.

Low fat doesn't mean low or no flavor. From chicken to beef, you'll find a variety of recipes tasty enough to please the pickiest palate.

What You'll Find in This Book

Thanks to the nutrition analyses provided in this book, it's easy to see the amount of fat, in grams, and the Percent Daily Value Fat in each recipe. This is a sample of all the Nutrition Facts listed with every recipe:

TOTAL FAT: 11 g
DAILY VALUE FAT: 17%
DAILY VALUE SATURATED FAT: 10%

NUTRITION FACTS
PER SERVING:

Calories	370
Total Fat	11 g
Saturated Fat	2g
Cholesterol	45 mg
Sodium	563
Carbohydrate	48 g
Fiber	2 g
Protein	22 g

Here, and on today's food labels, the Percent Daily Value Fat is based on 2,000 calories and 65 grams fat (including 20 grams saturated fat) each day. From the above example, you can see that this recipe includes 11 grams of fat (17% of the 65 fat grams for the day) and 2 grams saturated fat (10% of the 20 grams saturated fat for the day).

Mexican foods are taboo. Movie popcorn is a nibbling nightmare! Italian food? Forget it. If you read the newspaper, watch TV, or listen to the radio, you're bombarded with ever-changing food reports about fat and cholesterol. You may think that you have only two choices: Blissfully binge on your favorite no-no's and forget any advice or follow a fat-free diet and compromise taste, right? . . . Wrong.

Eating by the Numbers

In this book you'll find a collection of recipes that delivers on great taste and sound nutrition. To meet our standards for low fat, every recipe in *Low-Fat & Luscious* contains no more than 12 grams of fat. Generally, eating foods low in *total fat* will help reduce your daily intake of saturated fat and cholesterol—the true dietary villains in heart disease.

On average, your total fat intake over the course of a day should be limited to 30 percent of your *total calories*. If you apply the 30 percent guideline to single foods or recipes, (rather than total fat intake over the course of at least a day) you can be misled. Although a food with 30 percent calories from fat may seem attractive, it may not be your best choice overall. To illustrate, let's consider the examples in the chart at *right*.

If you follow the 30 percent guideline for these examples, you'll probably veto the salmon and vote for the spaghetti or the pie because they have a lower Percent Calories from Fat. Notice that the salmon, however, has the fewest calories of the three. Because the total number of calories is low, the Percent Calories from Fat is deceptively high. Choosing a food based only on the percentage of calories from fat can cause you to overlook the *total* calories, which still must be taken into consideration within a balanced diet. Things haven't changed. Eating more calories than you need still adds up to weight gain.

Percent Calories from Fat

Food	Calories	Fat (grams)	% Calories from Fat
Grilled salmon steak	180	10	50
Spaghetti with meatballs	520	18	31
A slice of cherry pie	415	12	26

Today's Easier-To-Live-With Alternative

The alternate approach that you will find in this book—and on today's food labels—is based on the total number of fat grams suggested for an *entire day.* This approach focuses your attention on Percent Daily Value Fat of the foods you eat over the course of a day, rather than Percent Calories from Fat for a single food. It's a more sensible approach to eating healthfully. To illustrate, let's use the same food examples, but base them on a standard 2,000-calorie-a-day diet and the 65 grams fat found on food labels (see chart, *below*).

Based on these percentages, which food would you choose now? The salmon looks like your best bet with cherry pie coming in second. And, when you consider total calories as well as fat, salmon wins the prize on both counts.

Percent Daily Value from Fat

Food	Calories	Fat (grams)	% Daily Value Fat
Grilled salmon steak	180	10	15
Spaghetti with meatballs	520	18	27
A slice of cherry pie	415	12	18

Let's face it. Your body only cares about the total number of fat grams (or calories) you eat over time. Your fat intake should ideally fall within 30 percent of total calories (see tip box *right, Determining Your Fat Budget*). But that doesn't mean you need to forfeit all of your favorite foods in favor of fat-free products and paltry servings of salad.

There are no good foods or bad foods in a healthful, balanced diet. The most important thing is to evaluate what you eat over the long run—at least a day's or even a week's time. Now found on food labels, here are some guidelines to shoot for :

● **Total fat**—30 percent or less of total calories (see *Sample Menu for a Day, page 8,* based on 2,000 calories and 65 grams fat);
● **Saturated fat**—no more than 10 percent of your total calorie intake (about 20 grams for 2,000 calories);
● **Dietary cholesterol**—300 mg or less per day.

Plan a fat and calorie budget, stick to it as best you can, and don't fret if, now and then, you eat more than your own personal limit. An *occasional* slice of your favorite chocolate cake is not taboo. To see how a T-bone steak can fit into a meal plan for a day, review the sample menu on *page 8.*

Determining Your Fat Budget

To translate 30 percent calories from fat to fat grams, take the number of calories you need in a day, multiply by 30 percent (or 0.3), then divide by 9:

Daily calories	Your Daily Fat Budget
1200	40 grams
1600	53 grams
1800	60 grams
2000	67 grams*

*Note: *Guidelines on food labels are based on 2,000 calories a day. The fat grams are rounded off to 65 on all food labels.*

Sample Menu for a Day

	Calories	Fat(g)
Breakfast		
Whole-grain cereal	162	1.2
1% milk (½ cup)	51	1.3
Banana	105	0.6
Orange juice	56	0.25
Lunch		
Turkey sandwich		
2 slices turkey meat	102	3.8
2 slices whole wheat		
bread	122	2.2
Mayonnaise (1 Tbsp.)	100	11.2
Tomato (2 slices)	2	0.0
Lettuce leaf	3	0.0
Vegetable soup (1 cup)	79	1.5
Saltine crackers (2)	26	0.6
1% milk (1 cup)	102	2.6
Mixed melon cup	28	0.2
Snack		
Apple	81	0.5
Supper		
Broiled lean T-bone (6 oz.)	366	18.0
Baked potato with sour		
cream (1 Tbsp.) and		
chives	247	2.7
Steamed broccoli flowerets		
(½ cup)	25	0.1
Dinner salad (1 cup)	18	0.0
Low-cal Italian dressing		
(2 Tbsp.)	14	0.0
Whole wheat roll	72	0.8
Margarine or butter (2 tsp.)	72	8.2
Red wine (4 ounces)	85	0.0
Dessert		
Ice milk (½ cup)	92	3.0
Total	2010	58.8 g
		26% fat

What's the Bottom Line?

No matter how you slice it, spread it, pour it, or fry it, fat in any form is still fat. Remember these fat pointers:

● All fats can contribute to heart disease. If you eat too much of any type, your risk of heart disease increases.
● All fats should be used sparingly; mono- or polyunsaturated fats should be substituted for saturated fat in your total diet when possible.
● Although your heart may care which type of fat you eat, your fat cells don't. Saturated, monounsaturated, and polyunsaturated fats all contain the same number of calories per gram. Consuming too much of any one of them contributes to weight gain.

● Children under the age of two should *not* limit fat intake. They need it for proper growth and development.
● Trans-fatty acids (see *Margarine: Better than Butter?, page 11*) may increase blood cholesterol, but in a typical diet, their level is low.
● Look for margarine made with unsaturated liquid vegetable oils as the first ingredient. Also, buy tub or liquid margarine or vegetable oil spreads. The softer the margarine, the more unsaturated it is.
● Buy liquid vegetable oils that are high in unsaturated fats. These include canola, corn, olive, safflower, sesame, soybean, peanut, and sunflower oils.

Family Approved?

If you're worried about whether your family will object to low-fat meals, follow these tips:

● Start slowly and with a lot of enthusiasm. Your family will find your excitement contagious.
● Experiment with a few new recipes at a time.
● Stick with traditional, familiar recipes. Make changes to them using the tips on *page 9, How We Zapped the Fat.*

● Try blending low-fat products with regular products during a transition period.
● Involve the family in meal planning to ensure interest in the new menu.
● Be realistic with your expectations. It takes time to break old habits, so you should expect some setbacks in the beginning. Your road to health will be a long, happy one with the delicious recipes found in this book.

How We Zapped the Fat

You may wonder how we cut the fat but kept the flavor in these recipes. When you pay attention to a few basic techniques, it's easy. Here's how:

● Trim all visible fat from meat or poultry.

● Skim fat from the cooking liquids, sauces, soups, and gravies.

● Remove the skin from poultry. (It's OK to remove the skin after cooking because the meat doesn't absorb much of the fat.)

● Limit serving sizes of meat, poultry, and fish to 3 ounces (about the same size as a deck of cards).

● Use small amounts of strongly flavored cheeses rather than large amounts of mild cheeses. You'll get more cheese flavor with fewer grams of fat and calories.

● Select fat-trimming cooking techniques, such as roasting, broiling, grilling, or microwaving.

● Substitute nonfat yogurt or sour cream for regular sour cream in salad dressings, as baked potato toppers, in baking, etc.

● Use skim milk in place of whole milk.

● Cook vegetables in small amounts of water or broth instead of sautéing in butter or margarine.

● Substitute cocoa powder, which contains no fat, for chocolate, which is high in fat.

● Omit the butter, margarine, or cooking oil called for in package directions for rice or pasta.

● Use evaporated skim milk in place of light or heavy cream in soups or sauces.

● Try nonstick cooking spray or a nonstick skillet for sautéing foods.

● Consider serving meatless meals occasionally.

● Substitute pureed fruits for some of the fat in baked products.

Zap fat and calories from recipes with healthy cooking methods such as:

● Broiling

● Grilling

● Micro-cooking

● Poaching

● Steaming

● Stir-frying (using minimal fat)

TEX MEX

Remember to focus on an entire day's worth of what you eat rather than on single foods or recipes. Just like today's food labels, the recipes in this book list fat percentages based on a standard 2,000-calorie-a-day plan.

Why Worry about Fat and Cholesterol?

First things first: Fat and cholesterol are not identical twins. In fact, they are very different in most respects. The key point for all of us to remember, however, is that both can raise blood cholesterol, which clogs the arteries to the heart and increases the risk of heart disease. Although cholesterol is important to many body functions, your liver makes all you need, so you don't need any from what you eat.

So, when making food choices, remember that dietary cholesterol is *only* found in foods that come from animals. Because of cholesterol's link to heart disease, health experts recommend that you limit your daily intake to no more than 300 mg per day.

The real bad-guy in this current web of worries about fat and cholesterol, however, is saturated fat (see *The Many Faces of Fat, below*). Saturated fat raises your blood cholesterol *more than anything else you eat*. It, too, is found in the greatest amounts in foods from animals. It also occurs in some vegetable oils. Sources include:

Bacon fat	Hydrogenated oils
Butter	Lard
Cocoa butter	Meat fat (beef, pork,
Coconut	poultry, or lamb)
Coconut oil	Palm kernel oil
Cream	Palm oil
Egg and egg-yolk solids	Vegetable shortenings
Hardened fat or oil	Whole-milk solids

The Many Faces of Fat

Saturated fat, the true dietary villain in heart disease, primarily hides in animal products, such as milk products and fatty meats, although it also takes refuge in some vegetable oils (such as coconut, palm, and palm kernel oils). Poultry, fish, and shellfish also contain some saturated fat but generally have less than meat.

Polyunsaturated fat, a fat that is kinder to your heart, is found in vegetable oils, such as corn, cottonseed, soybean, sesame, sunflower, and safflower. Fish oils, or omega-3 fatty acids, are also polyunsaturated and found abundantly in such cold-water fish as herring, tuna, salmon, and

mackerel. When this type of fat is *substituted* for saturated fats in the diet and consumed in limited quantities, it can help lower blood cholesterol. It is liquid at room temperature.

Monounsaturated fat has received broad coverage in the media. The Mediterranean diet, with its generous use of olive oil, would seem to be the answer. But don't be fooled. Although the family of olive, canola, and peanut oils is more healthful than other fats, it is not a cure-all. Like polyunsaturated fat, monounsaturated fat can help lower blood cholesterol if substituted for saturated fat in your diet.

Fat as Our Friend

Fat appears to be our curse and our blessing. This nutrient does have many useful roles, for it

● Transports the much needed fat-soluble vitamins A, D, E, and K through the body.
● Aids in the use of carbohydrate and protein.
● Supplies essential fatty acids needed for growth, healthy skin, and production of body-regulating hormones.
● Supplies a concentrated source of energy that is important for young children when their small tummies can't hold enough food to meet their high calorie needs.
● Gives flavor to food.
● Provides a satisfying texture to foods.

Despite these useful roles, when your diet is too high in fat, you gamble with your health. A high-fat diet is high in calories and can lead to weight gain. Eating foods lower in fat will help you eat fewer calories. But remember: *Low fat doesn't mean low calorie.*

Is Margarine Better Than Butter?

Most of us thought margarine was the answer to high-saturated-fat butter because it came from polyunsaturated oils. This may not be the case. Remember that saturated fat is solid at room temperature. So is margarine! A process called hydrogenation makes oils more solid at room temperature. In this process, however, trans-fatty acids are formed. These acids, which are actually naturally occurring substances in meat and dairy products, are being scrutinized by the health community. Although scientific studies are inconclusive, some evidence suggests that trans-fatty acids may increase blood cholesterol levels, just as saturated fats do.

Fortunately, this type of fat from all dietary sources comprise only 2 to 4 percent of our total calorie intake. By comparison, saturated fats comprise about 14 percent of that total.

So should you dump margarine for butter? Most experts don't believe there is enough evidence yet to suggest that trans-fatty acids are harmful. Your major concern should be to reduce *saturated fat* in your diet—since we all consume more of those than we should—and to cut back on all types of fats.

What's on the horizon? Scientists are now using techniques to genetically modify the polyunsaturated fatty acid content of oil seeds to reduce the need for hydrogenation in oils.

What Can I Eat?

There are lots of tasty things you can eat! Here are some examples:

● **Pasta, rice, dry peas, and beans**

● **Lean meats and poultry**

● **Fish and seafood**

● **Fruits and vegetables**

● **Whole-grain breads and cereals**

● **Low-fat dairy products**

● **100% fruit or vegetable juices**

● **Sorbets or sherbets**

● **Angel food cake**

● **Our Orange-Chocolate Cake,**

see recipe, page 152

Blueberry Coffee Cake, recipe page 15

Apple Cinnamon Bread,
recipe page 14

Breakfast Dishes

Breakfast-skippers, listen up. Research has shown that children who don't eat breakfast aren't able to concentrate as well, have shorter attention spans, and have lower test scores than children who do. How can anyone (adults included) expect to get up and go without fuel? Get your morning fill-up right here with Southwest Breakfast Strata, Refrigerator Bran Muffins, Ham and Egg Breakfast Casserole, or Hot Five-Grain Cereal with Honey Fruit. Now you can start your family's engines early everyday!

TOTAL FAT: 1 g
DAILY VALUE FAT: 2%
DAILY VALUE SATURATED FAT: 0%

NUTRITION FACTS
PER SERVING:

Calories	101
Total Fat	1 g
Saturated Fat	0 g
Cholesterol	0 mg
Sodium	29 mg
Carbohydrate	20 g
Fiber	1 g
Protein	3 g

EXCHANGES:

1½ Starch

PREPARATION TIME: 30 minutes
RISING TIME: 1½ hours
BAKING TIME: 25 minutes

Apple-Cinnamon Bread

Have this bread ready for your busy mornings when time is at a premium. Warm up a slice or two in the microwave and spread with apple butter for a real treat. (See photograph on pages 12 and 13.)

2½ to 3 cups all-purpose flour
　1　package active dry yeast
　⅔　cup skim milk
　2　tablespoons granulated sugar
　1　tablespoon cooking oil
　⅛　teaspoon salt
　¼　cup refrigerated or frozen egg product, thawed
　　　Nonstick spray coating
　¼　cup packed brown sugar
　1　teaspoon ground cinnamon
　1　medium cooking apple, finely chopped (1 cup)
　⅓　sifted powdered sugar (optional)
1½　teaspoons apple juice or skim milk (optional)

● In a medium mixer bowl combine *1 cup* of the flour and the yeast. In a small saucepan heat and stir the milk, granulated sugar, oil, and salt just till warm (120° to 130°). Add to flour mixture along with egg product. Beat with an electric mixer on low speed for 30 seconds, scraping bowl constantly. Beat on high speed for 3 minutes. Using a spoon, stir in as much of the remaining flour as you can.

● Turn dough out onto a lightly floured surface. Knead in enough of the remaining flour to make a moderately stiff dough that is smooth and elastic (6 to 8 minutes total). Shape into a ball. Place in a lightly greased bowl; turn once to grease surface. Cover and let rise in a warm place till double (about 1 hour).

● Punch dough down. Turn out onto a lightly floured surface. Cover and let dough rest for 10 minutes. Spray an 8x4x2-inch loaf pan with nonstick coating. Set aside. In a small mixing bowl, stir together brown sugar and cinnamon. Set aside. Roll dough into a 12x8-inch rectangle. Brush lightly with water. Sprinkle with the cinnamon mixture. Top with chopped apple. Roll up from one of the short sides. Seal edge and ends. Place, seam side down, in the prepared pan. Cover and let rise till almost double (about 30 minutes). Bake in a 375° oven for 25 to 30 minutes or till bread sounds hollow when tapped. To prevent overbrowning, cover loosely with foil during the last 10 to 15 minutes of baking. Remove from pan; cool on a wire rack.

● If desired, in a small bowl stir together powdered sugar and apple juice or milk. Drizzle over the top of the loaf. Makes 1 loaf (16 servings).

Blueberry Coffee Cake

Fresh berries make this coffee cake a winning breakfast treat, but unthawed frozen blueberries or raspberries are a delicious year-round alternative. (See photograph on page 12.)

1¼ cups all-purpose flour
½ cup granulated sugar
½ teaspoon baking powder
½ teaspoon baking soda
½ teaspoon ground cinnamon
⅛ teaspoon salt
⅔ cup buttermilk
1 beaten egg
3 tablespoons cooking oil
½ teaspoon vanilla
1 cup fresh or frozen blueberries
2 tablespoons brown sugar
1 tablespoon all-purpose flour
¼ teaspoon ground cinnamon
2 teaspoons margarine or butter

● Lightly grease and flour a 9x1-inch round baking pan. Set aside. In a large mixing bowl stir together the 1¼ cups flour, granulated sugar, baking powder, baking soda, the ½ teaspoon cinnamon, and the salt. In a small mixing bowl stir together buttermilk, egg, oil, and vanilla. Add to dry ingredients. Stir till smooth. Pour batter into prepared pan. Sprinkle berries over batter.

● In a small bowl combine the brown sugar, the 1 tablespoon flour, the ¼ teaspoon cinnamon, and the margarine or butter. Sprinkle over top of berries. Bake in a 350° oven for 30 to 35 minutes or till a toothpick inserted near the center comes out clean. To serve, cut into wedges. Serve warm. Makes 8 servings.

TOTAL FAT: **6 g**
DAILY VALUE FAT: **9%**
DAILY VALUE SATURATED FAT: **5%**

NUTRITION FACTS
PER SERVING:

Calories	200
Total Fat	6 g
Saturated Fat	1 g
Cholesterol	27 mg
Sodium	166 mg
Carbohydrate	33 g
Fiber	1 g
Protein	3 g

EXCHANGES:
2 Starch, 1 Fat

PREPARATION TIME: **20 minutes**
COOKING TIME: **30 minutes**

TOTAL FAT: 4 g
DAILY VALUE FAT: 6%
DAILY VALUE SATURATED FAT: 5%

NUTRITION FACTS
PER MUFFIN:

Calories	143
Total Fat	4 g
Saturated Fat	1 g
Cholesterol	0 mg
Sodium	241 mg
Carbohydrate	26 g
Fiber	3 g
Protein	4 g

EXCHANGES:
1½ Starch, 1 Fat

PREPARATION TIME: 15 minutes
CHILLING TIME: 2 hours
COOKING TIME: 18 minutes

Refrigerator Bran Muffins

Keep this convenient muffin batter in the refrigerator. Make as many muffins as you like when you want a fresh-baked breakfast or snack.

1½ cups packaged low-fat biscuit mix
1 cup whole bran cereal
1 teaspoon ground cinnamon
½ cup refrigerated or frozen egg product, thawed
1 cup skim milk
⅓ cup packed brown sugar
2 tablespoon cooking oil
¾ cup snipped dried fruit, such as cherries, raisins, or apricots

● In a large mixing bowl combine biscuit mix, cereal, and cinnamon. Make a well in the center. In a small bowl combine egg product, milk, brown sugar, and oil. Add egg mixture all at once to cereal mixture. Stir just till moistened (batter will be lumpy). Fold in fruit. To store, place batter in a covered container and chill at least 2 hours or up to 3 days.

● To bake, gently stir batter. Spray desired number of muffin cups with nonstick coating; fill cups ⅔ full. Bake in a 375° oven for 18 to 20 minutes or till golden. Remove from pans and cool on a wire rack. Makes 12 muffins.

Bring on the Bran

Bran is a good source of fiber, which helps ward off the risk of heart disease and some types of cancer. There are four types of bran, which come from grain kernels of corn, rice, oats, and wheat. Of the four types, corn has the highest fiber content. The muffin recipe, above, is an excellent source of bran, thanks to the cereal in the batter. Just ⅓ cup of whole bran cereal contains about 9 grams fiber.

Hot Five-Grain Cereal with Honey Fruit

This cereal makes 8 servings, but you can make it ahead, chill it, and reheat it in the microwave oven when you want a speedy breakfast for one.

6 cups water
½ cup regular brown rice
½ cup regular pearl barley
⅓ cup wheat berries
⅓ cup rye berries
⅓ cup millet
  Dash salt
½ cup orange juice or pineapple juice
¼ cup honey
2 cups sliced strawberries
1 medium banana, sliced

● In a large saucepan, heat the water to boiling; stir in the brown rice, barley, wheat berries, rye berries, millet, and salt. Return to boiling. Reduce heat. Simmer, covered, for 45 to 60 minutes or till grains are tender, stirring occasionally. (If mixture becomes too dry during cooking, stir in a small amount of additional water during cooking.)

● To serve, stir together the orange or pineapple juice and honey. Spoon hot cereal into serving bowls. Top each serving with some of the juice mixture, sliced strawberries, and banana. Makes 8 servings.

To make ahead: You may cover and chill the cooked cereal for up to 5 days. To reheat *1 serving* of chilled cereal, measure *¾ to 1 cup* cereal into a microwave-safe bowl. Cover with waxed paper; micro-cook on 100% power (high) for 1½ to 2 minutes or till heated through. To serve, stir together 1 tablespoon of the orange or pineapple juice and 1 teaspoon of the honey; drizzle mixture over hot cereal. Top with ¼ cup of the sliced strawberries and a few of the banana slices.

TOTAL FAT: 1 g
DAILY VALUE FAT: 2%
DAILY VALUE SATURATED FAT: 0%

NUTRITION FACTS
PER SERVING:

Calories	226
Total Fat	2 g
Saturated Fat	0 g
Cholesterol	0 mg
Sodium	26 mg
Carbohydrate	50 g
Fiber	5 g
Protein	6 g

EXCHANGES:

1½ Fruit, 2 Starch

PREPARATION TIME: 5 minutes
COOKING TIME: 45 minutes

Baked French Toast with Orange Syrup

Give each slice of bread just a quick dip in the egg mixture so you have enough for all 8 slices.

TOTAL FAT: 3 g
DAILY VALUE FAT: 5%
DAILY VALUE SATURATED FAT: 5%

NUTRITION FACTS
PER SERVING:

Calories	220
Total Fat	3 g
Saturated Fat	1 g
Cholesterol	54 mg
Sodium	358 mg
Carbohydrate	38 g
Fiber	0 g
Protein	9 g

EXCHANGES:
½ Fruit, 2 Starch, ½ Meat

PREPARATION TIME: 10 minutes
COOKING TIME: 11 minutes

Nonstick spray coating
1 slightly beaten egg
1 slightly beaten egg white
¾ cup skim milk
1 teaspoon vanilla
8 ½-inch-thick slices French bread
Orange Syrup
Orange slices (optional)
Strawberries (optional)

● Spray a large baking sheet with nonstick spray coating; set aside. In a shallow bowl combine the whole egg, egg white, milk, and vanilla. Dip bread slices in egg mixture just long enough to coat both sides. Place slices on the prepared baking sheet.

● Bake in a 450° oven about 6 minutes or till bread is lightly browned. Turn bread over and bake 5 to 8 minutes more or till golden. Serve toast with warm Orange Syrup. If desired, garnish with orange slices and strawberries. Makes 4 servings.

Orange Syrup: In a small saucepan stir together ¼ teaspoon *orange peel*, ⅔ cup *orange juice*, 1 tablespoon *honey*, 1½ teaspoons *cornstarch*, and ⅛ teaspoon ground *cinnamon*. Cook and stir till thickened and bubbly. Cook and stir for 2 minutes more.

Puffy Pineapple-Ham Pancake

Flip 'em no more! Just stir this pancake together and put it in the oven to bake.

TOTAL FAT: 5 g
DAILY VALUE FAT: 7%
DAILY VALUE SATURATED FAT: 5%

**NUTRITION FACTS
PER SERVING:**

Calories	194
Total Fat	5 g
Saturated Fat	1 g
Cholesterol	5 mg
Sodium	332 mg
Carbohydrate	28 g
Fiber	1 g
Protein	11 g

EXCHANGES:

1 Fruit, 1 Starch, 1 Meat

PREPARATION TIME: 15 minutes
COOKING TIME: 15 minutes

Nonstick spray coating
1 8-ounce can pineapple tidbits (juice pack), well drained
2 ounces lower-fat fully cooked ham, chopped
½ cup all-purpose flour
2 tablespoons brown sugar
½ teaspoon baking powder
½ teaspoon ground cinnamon
Dash ground nutmeg
¼ cup refrigerated or frozen egg product, thawed, or 1 beaten egg
⅔ cup skim milk
1 tablespoon margarine or butter, melted
½ teaspoon vanilla
3 egg whites
Light pancake and waffle syrup product (optional)

● Spray a 9-inch pie plate or four 12- to 16-ounce individual casseroles with nonstick coating. Sprinkle pineapple and ham on the bottom of the pie plate or casseroles; set aside.

● In a medium mixing bowl stir together flour, brown sugar, baking powder, cinnamon, and nutmeg. In a small mixing bowl combine the egg product or egg, skim milk, melted margarine or butter, and vanilla. Add egg mixture to dry ingredients. Stir just till combined.

● In a medium mixing bowl beat egg whites till stiff peaks form (tips stand straight). Gently fold flour mixture into beaten egg whites. Pour over pineapple and ham in the pie plate or casseroles. Bake in a 425° oven for 15 to 18 minutes or till puffed and lightly browned. If desired, serve with warm syrup. Makes 4 servings.

Ham and Egg Breakfast Casserole

Save time by assembling the casserole the night before and cooking it in the morning. Cover the uncooked casserole and place it in the refrigerator for 4 to 6 hours or overnight. Bake it, uncovered, in a 350° oven about 40 minutes or till it tests done.

1 large potato (8 ounces)
1 cup water
½ cup sliced fresh mushrooms
¼ cup chopped red sweet pepper
   (⅓ of a medium)
   Nonstick spray coating
⅓ cup evaporated skim milk
2 tablespoons all-purpose flour
2 8-ounce cartons refrigerated or frozen
   egg product, thawed
¼ cup sliced green onion
2 tablespoons snipped parsley
½ teaspoon dried marjoram, crushed
¼ teaspoon pepper
⅛ teaspoon salt
2 ounces lower-fat fully cooked ham,
   finely chopped
½ cup reduced-fat shredded cheddar cheese
   (2 ounces)

● Scrub potato. Thinly slice. In a medium saucepan combine potato, water, mushrooms, and red pepper. Bring to boiling. Reduce heat. Simmer, covered, about 8 minutes or till vegetables are tender. Drain well.

● Meanwhile, spray a 2-quart-square baking dish with nonstick coating; set aside. In a medium mixing bowl gradually stir milk into the flour. Stir in egg product, green onion, parsley, marjoram, pepper, and salt. Arrange cooked potato mixture on the bottom of the prepared baking dish. Sprinkle with ham. Pour the egg mixture over all. Bake in a 350° oven for 20 to 25 minutes or till a knife inserted near center comes out clean. Sprinkle with cheese. Return to oven for 1 minute to melt cheese. To serve, cut into squares. Makes 6 servings.

TOTAL FAT: 5 g
DAILY VALUE FAT: 8%
DAILY VALUE SATURATED FAT: 10%

NUTRITION FACTS
PER SERVING:

Calories	167
Total Fat	5 g
Saturated Fat	2 g
Cholesterol	11 mg
Sodium	372 mg
Carbohydrate	13 g
Fiber	1 g
Protein	16 g

EXCHANGES:
1 Starch, 2 Meat

PREPARATION TIME: 25 minutes
COOKING TIME: 20 minutes

Lemon-Poppy Seed Pancakes

A honey-sweetened raspberry sauce makes these pancakes extra special. When fresh berries aren't in season, use frozen loose-pack raspberries.

1   **cup all-purpose flour**
1   **tablespoon sugar**
2   **teaspoons baking powder**
¼   **teaspoon baking soda**
¼   **teaspoon salt**
1   **8-ounce carton lemon low-fat yogurt**
¾   **cup skim milk**
¼   **cup refrigerated or frozen egg product, thawed, or 1 egg**
1   **tablespoon poppy seed**
    Raspberry Sauce
    Fresh raspberries (optional)
    Orange curl (optional)

● For pancakes, in a medium mixing bowl stir together the flour, sugar, baking powder, baking soda, and salt. In another mixing bowl, combine the yogurt, milk, egg product or egg, and poppy seed; add to the flour mixture all at once. Stir the mixture just till combined but still slightly lumpy.

● For each pancake, pour about ¼ *cup* batter onto a hot, lightly greased or nonstick griddle or heavy skillet. Cook till pancakes are golden brown on both sides, turning when pancakes have bubbly surfaces and slightly dry edges. Serve pancakes with warm Raspberry Sauce. If desired, garnish with additional fresh raspberries and an orange curl. Makes 6 servings (12 pancakes).

Raspberry Sauce: In a small saucepan stir together ¼ cup *orange juice*, 2 tablespoons *honey*, and 2 teaspoons *cornstarch*. Add 1 cup *fresh raspberries or frozen raspberries,* thawed. Cook and stir over medium heat till thickened and bubbly. Cook and stir for 2 minutes more. Strain through a sieve to remove seeds.

TOTAL FAT: 2 g
DAILY VALUE FAT: 3%
DAILY VALUE SATURATED FAT: 3%

**NUTRITION FACTS
PER SERVING:**

Calories	184
Total Fat	2 g
Saturated Fat	0 g
Cholesterol	2 mg
Sodium	320 mg
Carbohydrate	36 g
Fiber	2 g
Protein	6 g

EXCHANGES:

½ Fruit, 2 Starch

PREPARATION TIME: 15 minutes
COOKING TIME: 40 minutes

TOTAL FAT: **4 g**
DAILY VALUE FAT: **6%**
DAILY VALUE SATURATED FAT: **0%**

NUTRITION FACTS
PER SERVING:

Calories	175
Total Fat	4 g
Saturated Fat	0 g
Cholesterol	9 mg
Sodium	413 mg
Carbohydrate	24 g
Fiber	1 g
Protein	12 g

EXCHANGES:

1 Meat, 1½ Starch

PREPARATION TIME: **20 minutes**
COOKING TIME: **30 minutes**
STANDING TIME: **10 minutes**

Savory Brunch Strudel

Score the phyllo before baking so it doesn't shatter when the strudel is sliced.

1 cup fat-free or low-fat ricotta cheese
¼ cup freshly shredded Asiago or Parmesan cheese
2 tablespoons snipped fresh dill or 1 teaspoon dried dillweed
1 ounce chopped lower-fat fully cooked ham
1 2-ounce jar diced pimiento, drained
2 tablespoons thinly sliced green onion
1 slightly beaten egg white
¼ teaspoon salt
¼ teaspoon pepper
8 ounces asparagus, cut into ½-inch pieces or ½ of a 10-ounce package frozen cut asparagus
10 sheets frozen phyllo dough, thawed Butter-flavor nonstick spray coating
¼ cup fine dry bread crumbs

● In a large bowl combine ricotta cheese, Asiago or Parmesan cheese, dill, ham, pimiento, green onion, egg white, salt, and pepper; set aside.

● Cook asparagus covered, in a small amount of boiling water for 4 to 5 minutes or just till crisp-tender (don't overcook). Drain. Cool under cold water. Stir into ricotta mixture.

● Spray a large baking sheet with nonstick coating; set aside. Place 1 sheet of phyllo on a dry kitchen towel (keep remaining phyllo covered with a damp kitchen towel to prevent drying out). Spray with nonstick coating. Place another sheet of phyllo atop. Spray with nonstick coating. Sprinkle with *one-fourth* of the bread crumbs. Repeat with remaining sheets and remaining bread crumbs. Spray last layer with nonstick coating.

● Spoon cheese mixture lengthwise onto half of the top layer of phyllo, leaving about a 1½-inch border on all sides. Fold in the short sides over the filling. Starting from a long side, roll up layers jelly-roll style.

● Place strudel, seam side down, on the prepared baking sheet. Spray top with nonstick coating. Using a sharp knife, score into 12 slices, cutting through the top layer only. If desired, sprinkle with additional bread crumbs. Bake in a 375° oven for 30 minutes or till light brown. Let stand for 10 minutes before serving. To serve, cut along scored lines into slices. Makes 6 servings.

TOTAL FAT: **2 g**
DAILY VALUE FAT: **3%**
DAILY VALUE SATURATED FAT: **0%**

NUTRITION FACTS
PER SERVING:

Calories	162
Total Fat	2 g
Saturated Fat	0 g
Cholesterol	5 mg
Sodium	81 mg
Carbohydrate	26 g
Fiber	1 g
Protein	11 g

EXCHANGES:

1 Fruit, 1 Starch, 1 Meat

PREPARATION TIME: **35 minutes**
COOKING TIME: **15 minutes**

Cheese Blintzes with Apricot Sauce

For make-ahead convenience, fill, fold, and refrigerate the blintzes for up to 24 hours. Then, bake them, covered, in a 350° oven about 25 minutes or till heated through.

⅔ cup skim milk
⅓ cup all-purpose flour
3 tablespoons refrigerated or frozen egg product, thawed
1 teaspoon cooking oil
  Nonstick spray coating
¾ cup fat-free ricotta cheese
2 tablespoons refrigerated or frozen egg product, thawed
2 tablespoons powdered sugar
½ teaspoon finely shredded orange peel or lemon peel

● For crepes, in a small mixing bowl stir together milk, flour, the 3 tablespoons egg product, and oil. Beat with a rotary beater or wire whisk till well combined. Spray a 6-inch nonstick skillet with nonstick coating. Heat over medium heat. Remove from heat. Spoon about *2 tablespoons* of the batter into the skillet; lift and tilt skillet to spread batter. Return skillet to heat; brown on one side only (about 30 to 60 seconds). (Or, cook on an inverted crepe maker according to manufacturer's directions.) Invert pan over paper towels; remove crepe. Repeat with remaining batter, making 8 crepes total. (Note: Spraying a hot pan with nonstick coating is not recommended. If necessary, lightly brush the skillet with cooking oil to prevent crepes from sticking.)

● Spray a 2-quart-rectangular baking dish with nonstick coating; set aside. For filling, in a medium bowl stir together the ricotta cheese, the 2 tablespoons egg product, the 2 tablespoons powdered sugar, and the orange or lemon peel. Spoon about *1 rounded tablespoon* of mixture into the center of the unbrowned side of a crepe. Fold lower edge of crepe up and over filling. Fold in sides, just till they meet. Roll up crepe from lower edge. Repeat with remaining crepes and filling. Place filled blintzes in prepared baking dish. Bake, covered, in a 350° oven for 15 to 20 minutes or till heated through. To serve, place 2 blintzes on a serving plate; spoon Apricot Sauce over each serving. Makes 4 servings.

Apricot Sauce: In a small saucepan combine one 5½-ounce can (⅔ cup) *apricot nectar or orange juice,* 1 tablespoon *powdered sugar,* and 2 teaspoons *cornstarch.* Cook and stir over medium heat till thickened and bubbly. Cook and stir for 2 minutes more. Stir in ½ cup *fresh or frozen blueberries,* thawed. Heat through.

Southwest Breakfast Strata

Avoid the last-minute morning rush. Simply assemble this tasty egg dish the night before, then bake it in the morning.

2   slices Canadian-style bacon
    Nonstick spray coating
8   ½-inch-thick slices French bread or other
    firm-textured bread
1½ cups refrigerated or frozen egg product,
    thawed
2   tablespoons diced green chili peppers,
    drained
⅛   teaspoon pepper
2   plum tomatoes, thinly sliced
2   ounces reduced-fat Monterey Jack
    cheese, shredded (½ cup)
1   tablespoon snipped cilantro

● Cut the Canadian-style bacon into thin strips; set aside. Spray a 2-quart-rectangular baking dish with nonstick coating. Place bread slices on the bottom of the prepared baking dish, cutting to fit the dish.

● In a medium mixing bowl stir together the egg product, chili peppers, and pepper. Pour egg mixture over bread. Sprinkle Canadian bacon over egg mixture. Arrange tomato slices atop bacon. Sprinkle with the cheese. Cover; chill for several hours or overnight. Bake, uncovered, in a 350° oven about 25 minutes or till a knife inserted near the center comes out clean. Before serving, sprinkle with cilantro. Makes 6 servings.

TOTAL FAT: 6 g
DAILY VALUE FAT: 9%
DAILY VALUE SATURATED FAT: 10%

**NUTRITION FACTS
PER SERVING:**

Calories	189
Total Fat	6 g
Saturated Fat	2 g
Cholesterol	11 mg
Sodium	494 mg
Carbohydrate	19 g
Fiber	0 g
Protein	15 g

EXCHANGES:
1½ Starch, 1½ Meat

PREPARATION TIME: 15 minutes
CHILLING TIME: 4 to 12 hours
COOKING TIME: 25 minutes

Battle of the Bacon

Canadian-style bacon makes a lean substitute for regular bacon. Compare the two and see how many fat grams and calories you can save:

	Fat (grams)	Calories
1 slice Canadian-style bacon (1 ounce)	2	45
4 slices cooked bacon (1 ounce)	13	145

Crispy Chicken Bites, recipe page 31

Vegetable Pizza,
recipe page 30

Snacks & Appetizers

Mom may have told you not to eat between meals, but snacks and nibbles aren't necessarily taboo. Just make sure you choose wisely. Here you'll find a mix of tasty recipes for snacking and entertaining. Choose from Roasted Garlic and Cheese Appetizers, Curried Crab Dip, Apricot-Cardamom Bars . . . even Fudge Brownies. They've all been lightened up to help you cut down on calories and fat. So, go ahead—nibble away!

TOTAL FAT: 5 g
DAILY VALUE FAT: 8%
DAILY VALUE SATURATED FAT: 10%

**NUTRITION FACTS
PER SERVING:**

Calories	105
Total Fat	5 g
Saturated Fat	2 g
Cholesterol	7 mg
Sodium	235 mg
Carbohydrate	13 g
Fiber	1 g
Protein	3 g

EXCHANGES:
½ Starch, 1 Fat

PREPARATION TIME: 25 minutes
COOKING TIME: 12 minutes

Vegetable Pizza

This cold appetizer pizza has a cream cheese layer topped with lots of colorful vegetables that add fiber and vitamins to your snack. (See photograph pages 28 and 29.)

Nonstick spray coating
1 package (8) refrigerated buttermilk biscuits
½ of an 8-ounce package reduced-fat cream cheese (Neufchâtel), softened
¼ cup reduced-calorie or nonfat mayonnaise dressing or salad dressing
½ teaspoon dried dillweed
⅛ teaspoon onion powder
⅛ teaspoon garlic powder
¾ cup chopped fresh spinach
½ of a 7-ounce jar roasted red sweet peppers, drained and chopped (about ⅓ cup), or ⅓ cup diced pimiento, drained
2 cups desired fresh vegetables, such as broccoli flowerets, sliced carrot, jicama strips, sliced green onions, green sweet pepper strips, sliced and quartered yellow summer squash or zucchini, and/or cauliflower flowerets

● Spray a 12-inch pizza pan with nonstick spray coating. For crust, place 7 biscuits in the pan near the edge forming a circle; place 1 biscuit in the center. Using fingers, press the biscuits into the pan to form a single crust. Bake in a 375° oven for 12 to 15 minutes or till light brown. Cool in pan.

● Meanwhile, in a medium mixing bowl stir together cream cheese, mayonnaise or salad dressing, dillweed, onion powder, and garlic powder. Add spinach and roasted peppers or pimiento, stirring just till combined.

● Spread the cream cheese mixture onto the cooled crust. Arrange vegetables atop cream cheese mixture. To serve, cut into wedges. Serve immediately. Or, cover and chill for up to 24 hours. Makes 12 servings.

Crispy Chicken Bites

Need a quick-serve party appetizer? These cracker-coated, bite-size nuggets bake in the oven in less than 15 minutes. (See photograph page 28.)

- 1 **pound skinless, boneless chicken thighs or breasts**
- ¼ **cup all-purpose flour**
- 1 **teaspoon dried parsley flakes**
- ½ **teaspoon poultry seasoning**
- ⅛ **teaspoon salt**
- **Dash pepper**
- 1 **beaten egg**
- 2 **tablespoons skim milk**
- 1¼ **cup finely crushed wheat crackers (about 30)**
- **Fruit Dipping Sauce**

● Rinse chicken. Pat dry with paper towels. Cut the chicken into 1-inch pieces. In a plastic bag combine the flour, dried parsley, poultry seasoning, salt, and pepper. Add the chicken pieces, a few at a time, to the seasoned flour mixture. Close the bag and shake to coat chicken pieces well. Set chicken aside.

● In a small mixing bowl combine the beaten egg and milk. In another small bowl place the finely crushed crackers. Dip the flour-coated chicken pieces, *one-fourth* of the pieces at a time, into the egg-and-milk mixture. Roll the chicken pieces in the crushed crackers. Place the coated chicken pieces in a single layer on a large ungreased baking sheet. Bake in a 400° oven for 10 to 12 minutes or till chicken pieces are no longer pink. Serve with dipping sauce. Makes 8 servings.

Fruit Dipping Sauce: In a small saucepan combine one 10-ounce jar *spreadable fruit,* such as grape, black cherry, or strawberry, 2 tablespoons *lemon juice,* ⅛ teaspoon ground *mace,* and dash ground *cloves.* Cook and stir over medium heat till heated through. Serve with Crispy Chicken Bites. Makes about 1½ cups.

TOTAL FAT: 5 g
DAILY VALUE FAT: 6%
DAILY VALUE SATURATED FAT: 5%

NUTRITION FACTS PER SERVING:

Calories	145
Total Fat	5 g
Saturated Fat	1 g
Cholesterol	57 mg
Sodium	73 mg
Carbohydrate	23 g
Fiber	0 g
Protein	13 g

EXCHANGES:
½ **Starch, 2 Meat**

PREPARATION TIME: 25 minutes
COOKING TIME: 10 minutes

Marinated Zucchini and Mushrooms

This light lemon-flavored dressing perks up fresh vegetables for a refreshing appetizer. Use any other herb you like, such as basil, thyme, or mint, for a change in flavor.

TOTAL FAT: 3 g
DAILY VALUE FAT: 5%
DAILY VALUE SATURATED FAT: 0%

**NUTRITION FACTS
PER SERVING:**

Calories	41
Total Fat	3 g
Saturated Fat	0 g
Cholesterol	0 mg
Sodium	55 mg
Carbohydrate	4 g
Fiber	1 g
Protein	1 g

EXCHANGES:

1 Vegetable, ½ Fat

PREPARATION TIME: 20 minutes
MARINATING TIME: 8 hours

8 ounces small whole fresh mushrooms
     (3 cups)
2 small zucchini and/or yellow summer
     squash, bias-sliced into ½-inch-thick
     slices (2 cups)
1 small red sweet pepper, cut into square
     pieces (½ cup)
1 clove garlic, minced
¼ cup lemon juice
2 tablespoons olive oil or vegetable oil
1 tablespoon sugar
¼ teaspoon salt
¼ teaspoon dried tarragon or oregano,
     crushed
¼ teaspoon pepper

● In a plastic bag set in a large bowl place mushrooms, zucchini and/or yellow summer squash, and red pepper.

● For marinade, in small mixing bowl stir together garlic, lemon juice, oil, sugar, salt, tarragon or oregano, and pepper. Pour marinade over vegetables in bag; seal bag. Marinate vegetables in the refrigerator for 8 hours or overnight, turning bag occasionally.

● To serve, pour vegetables and marinade into a serving dish. Serve with toothpicks. Makes about 8 servings.

Fiesta Shrimp Appetizer

For even more heat, substitute 2 to 4 tablespoons chopped jalapeño pepper for the anaheim pepper.

2 **pounds fresh or frozen large shrimp,**
  in shells
2 **cloves garlic, minced**
½ **teaspoon finely shredded lime peel**
¼ **cup lime juice**
2 **tablespoons olive oil**
2 **tablespoons finely chopped green onion**
¼ **cup chopped fresh anaheim pepper**
1 **to 2 tablespoons snipped cilantro or**
  parsley
½ **teaspoon sugar**
½ **teaspoon salt**
¼ **teaspoon pepper**
  Lettuce leaves (optional)
1 **medium papaya and/or mango, peeled,**
  seeded, and sliced (optional)

● Thaw shrimp, if frozen. Peel and devein shrimp. In a medium saucepan bring 4 cups *water* to boiling. Add shrimp. Simmer, uncovered, for 1 to 3 minutes or till shrimp turn pink, stirring occasionally. Rinse under cold running water; drain. Set aside.

● In a heavy plastic bag set in a medium bowl combine garlic, lime peel, lime juice, olive oil, onion, anaheim pepper, cilantro or parsley, sugar, salt, and pepper; mix well. Place cooked shrimp in the bag. Turn bag to coat shrimp with marinade mixture. Marinate in the refrigerator for 2 to 3 hours, turning the bag occasionally.

● To serve, drain the shrimp, discarding the marinade. If desired, arrange papaya or mango slices around outer edge of a lettuce-lined serving platter. Place shrimp in center of platter. Makes 6 servings.

TOTAL FAT: 4 g
DAILY VALUE FAT: 6%
DAILY VALUE SATURATED FAT: 0%

NUTRITION FACTS
PER SERVING:

Calories	112
Total Fat	4 g
Saturated Fat	0 g
Cholesterol	174 mg
Sodium	288 mg
Carbohydrate	2 g
Fiber	0 g
Protein	18 g

EXCHANGES:
2½ Meat

PREPARATION TIME: 10 minutes
MARINATING TIME: 2 hours

TOTAL FAT: **2 g**
DAILY VALUE FAT: **3%**
DAILY VALUE SATURATED FAT: **0%**

NUTRITION FACTS
PER 2 PARTY BREAD SLICES
AND 1 TABLESPOON SPREAD:

Calories	67
Total Fat	2 g
Saturated Fat	0 g
Cholesterol	1 mg
Sodium	176 mg
Carbohydrate	9 g
Fiber	0 g
Protein	3 g

EXCHANGES:
½ **Starch,** ½ **Fat**

PREPARATION TIME: **30 minutes**
COOKING TIME: **35 minutes**

Roasted Garlic and Cheese Appetizers

For this simple appetizer, spread a creamy low-fat yogurt dip onto rye bread and add your choice of toppers.

1 **medium head garlic**
2 **teaspoons olive oil**
1 **cup dry curd cottage cheese**
¼ **cup plain low-fat yogurt**
⅓ **cup chopped walnuts, toasted**
2 **tablespoons snipped parsley**
¾ **teaspoon lemon-pepper seasoning**
¼ **teaspoon salt**
Rye party bread or firm, dark rye bread, sliced
Toppers, such as slices of beets, cucumber, pear, apple, pickles, ham, smoked salmon, lemon slice quarters, chives, crabmeat, dill sprigs, and/or chopped toasted walnuts

● Peel away the dry outer layers of skin from garlic, leaving cloves and skins intact. Cut off the pointed top portion (about ¼ inch), leaving the bulb intact but exposing the individual cloves. Place the head of garlic, cut side up, in a small baking dish. Drizzle olive oil over garlic.

● Bake, covered, in a 400° oven for 35 to 45 minutes or till cloves feel soft when pressed. Allow the bulb to cool. To remove the paste from the garlic head, squeeze the paste from each clove. Discard the skins. You should have about 1 tablespoon garlic paste.

● In a blender container combine the garlic paste, cottage cheese, yogurt, walnuts, parsley, lemon-pepper seasoning, and salt. Cover and blend till smooth. Spread cheese mixture onto rye bread slices; add desired toppers. Makes about 20 servings.

A Toast to Nuts

Toasting nuts not only brings out their flavor, but it also keeps them crisp when used in sauces or other moist mixtures.

To toast nuts, place them in a shallow baking pan; bake in a 400° oven for 7 to 8 minutes or till they start to brown. Make more than you need, then freeze them in an airtight container for later use.

Curried Crab Dip

It is important to drain the yogurt to give this dip its thick, creamy texture. Also make sure that the yogurt does not have gelatin in its ingredient list.

2   8-ounce cartons plain fat-free yogurt (without gelatin)
1   cup cooked crabmeat (6 ounces)
2   tablespoons chopped green onion
1   to 2 tablespoons snipped chutney
1   teaspoon curry powder
¼   teaspoon salt
    Dash ground red pepper
2   tablespoons sliced almonds, toasted (optional)
    Assorted crackers

● Line a large strainer with a double thickness of 100% cotton cheesecloth and place it over a medium mixing bowl. Spoon the yogurt into the strainer. Cover and refrigerate overnight. Discard any liquid in the bowl; clean the bowl.

● In the same mixing bowl combine the drained yogurt, crabmeat, green onion, chutney, curry powder, salt, and red pepper. Cover and chill till serving time or for up to 4 hours. Place mixture in a serving bowl. If desired, garnish with toasted sliced almonds. Serve with assorted crackers. Makes about 16 servings.

TOTAL FAT: 0 g
DAILY VALUE FAT: 0%
DAILY VALUE SATURATED FAT: 0%

**NUTRITION FACTS
PER TABLESPOON DIP:**

Calories	31
Total Fat	0 g
Saturated Fat	0 g
Cholesterol	10 mg
Sodium	90 mg
Carbohydrate	3 g
Fiber	0 g
Protein	4 g

EXCHANGES:
½ Meat

**DRAINING TIME FOR YOGURT: 8 hours
PREPARATION TIME: 5 minutes
CHILLING TIME: 4 hours**

Sweet Red Pepper Spread

Roasted red sweet peppers make a robust topper for Baked Pita Chips (see recipe below) or toasted slices of French bread.

TOTAL FAT: 1 g
DAILY VALUE FAT: 0%
DAILY VALUE SATURATED FAT: 0%

**NUTRITION FACTS
PER SERVING:**

Calories	63
Total Fat	1 g
Saturated Fat	0 g
Cholesterol	0 mg
Sodium	153 mg
Carbohydrate	13 g
Fiber	0 g
Protein	2 g

EXCHANGES:

1 Starch

PREPARATION TIME: 20 minutes
COOKING TIME: 40 minutes

2 medium red sweet peppers or
    one 7-ounce jar roasted red sweet
    peppers, drained
2 tablespoons tomato paste
1 teaspoon sugar
1 teaspoon snipped fresh thyme or
    ¼ teaspoon dried thyme, crushed
¼ teaspoon salt
⅛ teaspoon garlic powder
    Dash ground red pepper
    Baked Pita Chips

● To roast fresh peppers, cut into quarters lengthwise; remove seeds and stems. Line a baking sheet with foil. Place peppers, skin side up, on baking sheet, pressing to lie flat. Bake in a 425° oven for 20 minutes or till dark and blistered. Remove from oven and place in a clean paper bag. Close bag and let stand about 10 minutes. When cool enough to handle, peel the dark skins from peppers; discard skins.

● Place roasted peppers in a blender container or food processor bowl. Cover; blend or process till chopped fine. Add the tomato paste, sugar, thyme, salt, garlic powder, and ground red pepper. Cover; blend till nearly smooth. To serve, spread on Baked Pita Chips. To store leftovers, cover and refrigerate for up to 1 week. Makes about ¾ cup (12 servings).

Baked Pita Chips: Split 4 large *pita bread rounds* in half horizontally. Lightly spray the cut side of each pita bread half with *nonstick coating.* Sprinkle lightly with ½ to ¾ teaspoon *onion or garlic powder or pepper.* Cut each half into 6 wedges. Spread wedges in a single layer on a baking sheet. (You'll need to bake chips in batches.) Bake in a 350° oven for 10 to 12 minutes or till crisp. Serve with Sweet Red Pepper Spread. To store, place Baked Pita Chips in an airtight container for up to 1 week.

TOTAL FAT: 3 g
DAILY VALUE FAT: 5%
DAILY VALUE SATURATED FAT: 0%

NUTRITION FACTS
PER BROWNIE:

Calories	108
Total Fat	3 g
Saturated Fat	0 g
Cholesterol	0 mg
Sodium	42 mg
Carbohydrate	19 g
Fiber	0 g
Protein	2 g

EXCHANGES:
1 Starch, ½ Fat

PREPARATION TIME: 10 minutes
COOKING TIME: 20 minutes

Fudge Brownies

Use regular margarine, not a diet type, in this recipe. Products labeled spread, whipped, light, or diet all contain more water or air and less fat by volume. They can make some baked goods less tender.

Nonstick spray coating
1 cup all-purpose flour
1 cup packed brown sugar
¾ cup granulated sugar
½ cup unsweetened cocoa powder
½ teaspoon baking powder
½ cup refrigerated or frozen egg product, thawed
⅓ cup unsweetened applesauce
¼ cup margarine or butter, melted
1 teaspoon vanilla
¼ cup chopped pecans
1 tablespoon powdered sugar or chocolate-flavored syrup (optional)

● Spray a 3-quart-rectangular baking pan with nonstick coating. Set aside. In a large mixing bowl stir together flour, brown sugar, granulated sugar, cocoa powder, and baking powder. Stir in the egg product, applesauce, margarine or butter, and vanilla just till combined. Spread into the prepared pan. Sprinkle with pecans. Bake in a 350° oven about 20 minutes or till center appears set. Cool on a wire rack. If desired, sprinkle with powdered sugar or drizzle with chocolate-flavored syrup. To serve, cut into bars. Makes 24 brownies.

Cocoa Power

For delectable low-fat chocolate desserts, cocoa is your best friend. While an ounce of chocolate contains as much as 16 grams of fat per ounce, a comparable amount of cocoa powder has only 3 grams. To substitute cocoa powder for chocolate in baking, use 3 tablespoons unsweetened cocoa powder plus 1 tablespoon of water in place of each 1-ounce square of unsweetened chocolate. If the recipe calls for semisweet chocolate, also add 1 tablespoon sugar for each ounce of chocolate.

Date-Nut Bread

This date-filled bread has no added sugar or fat, and not a speck of cholesterol. What it does have is 3 grams of fiber, over 10 percent of your needs for the day.

1 **8-ounce package pitted whole dates, snipped**
1 **cup raisins**
1½ **cups boiling water**
2 **cups whole wheat flour**
1 **teaspoon baking soda**
1 **teaspoon baking powder**
¼ **teaspoon salt**
2 **slightly beaten egg whites**
1 **teaspoon vanilla**
½ **cup chopped almonds**

In a medium mixing bowl combine dates and raisins. Pour boiling water over mixture. Set aside to soften fruit and to cool slightly.

Lightly grease a 9x5x3-inch loaf pan; set aside. In a large mixing bowl stir together the flour, baking soda, baking powder, and salt. Stir the egg whites and vanilla into the cooled date mixture. Add the date mixture and the almonds to the flour mixture; stir till well combined (mixture will be thick).

Spoon batter evenly into a prepared pan. Bake in 350° oven for 40 to 50 minutes or till a toothpick inserted near the center of loaf comes out clean. Cool in pan for 10 minutes. Remove from pan; cool thoroughly on a wire rack. Wrap loaf tightly with plastic wrap and store overnight before serving. Makes 1 loaf (18 servings).

TOTAL FAT: 2 g
DAILY VALUE FAT: 3%
DAILY VALUE SATURATED FAT: 0%

NUTRITION FACTS PER SERVING:

Calories	123
Total Fat	2 g
Saturated Fat	0 g
Cholesterol	0 mg
Sodium	128 mg
Carbohydrate	26 g
Fiber	3 g
Protein	3 g

EXCHANGES:
½ Fruit, 1 Starch

PREPARATION TIME: 15 minutes
COOKING TIME: 40 minutes
HOLDING TIME: 8 hours

Apricot-Cardamom Bars

Applesauce and apricot nectar replace some of the fat in these moist snack bars.

1 cup all-purpose flour
½ cup packed brown sugar
½ teaspoon baking powder
¼ teaspoon baking soda
¼ teaspoon ground cardamom or
   ⅛ teaspoon ground cloves
1 slightly beaten egg
½ cup apricot nectar or orange juice
¼ cup unsweetened applesauce
2 tablespoons cooking oil
½ cup finely snipped dried apricots
Apricot Icing

● In a medium mixing bowl stir together flour, brown sugar, baking powder, baking soda, and cardamom or cloves; set aside. In a small mixing bowl stir together egg, apricot nectar or orange juice, applesauce, and oil till combined. Add to dry ingredients, stirring till just combined. Stir in the snipped apricots.

● Spread batter in an ungreased 11x7x1½-inch baking pan. Bake in a 350° oven about 25 minutes or till a toothpick inserted near the center comes out clean. Cool in pan on a wire rack. Drizzle with Apricot Icing. Cut into bars. Makes 24 bars.

Apricot Icing: In a small mixing bowl stir together ½ cup *powdered sugar* and 2 to 3 teaspoons *apricot nectar or orange juice.*

Try a Little Cardamom

Spices give food more life. Experiment with cardamom for a new change of spice. Cardamom pods are the fruit of a plant in the ginger family. Each pod contains clusters of tiny, hard, black seeds. It has a pungent and aromatic flowery sweetness that's a little like ginger but is much more subtle. Try it in place of some of your favorite spices, such as cinnamon, nutmeg, or ginger. Look for whole cardamom pods, whole seeds, and ground cardamom seeds in the spice section of your supermarket.

TOTAL FAT: 1 g
DAILY VALUE FAT: 2%
DAILY VALUE SATURATED FAT: 0%

NUTRITION FACTS
PER BAR:

Calories	63
Total Fat	1 g
Saturated Fat	0 g
Cholesterol	9 mg
Sodium	25 mg
Carbohydrate	12 g
Fiber	1 g
Protein	1 g

EXCHANGES:
1 Starch

PREPARATION TIME: 20 minutes
COOKING TIME: 25 minutes

Grilled Chicken and Vegetable Kabobs,
recipe page 46

Jalapeño Shrimp and Pasta,
recipe page 47

Main Dishes

"What's for dinner?" you ask. In this chapter, you'll discover convenient answers with a variety of updated dishes and new recipes that'll quickly become family favorites. Try the Spicy Beef and Bean Burgers, Chicken Fingers with Honey Sauce, Pasta with Basil Cream Sauce, or Jamaican Jerk Chicken. Choose any of these dishes knowing that they're as good for you and your family as they are great in taste.

TOTAL FAT: **4 g**
DAILY VALUE FAT: **6%**
DAILY VALUE SATURATED FAT: **5%**

NUTRITION FACTS
PER SERVING:

Calories	183
Total Fat	4 g
Saturated Fat	1 g
Cholesterol	59 mg
Sodium	314 mg
Carbohydrate	15 g
Fiber	1 g
Protein	23 g

EXCHANGES:

3 Meat, ½ Fruit, 1 Vegetable

PREPARATION TIME: **20 minutes**
COOKING TIME: **10 minutes**

Grilled Chicken and Vegetable Kabobs

If you place the vegetables and chicken on separate skewers, you won't have to worry about the vegetables becoming overcooked before the chicken is done—just remove each skewer from the grill when it is perfectly cooked. (See photograph page 44.)

1 **pound skinless, boneless chicken breast halves**
4 **medium fresh mushrooms**
3 **green onions, cut into 1-inch pieces**
1 **medium red, yellow, orange, and/or green sweet pepper, cut into 1½-inch pieces**
½ **cup salsa catsup**
2 **tablespoons jalapeño jelly**
  Hot cooked rice (optional)
  Thinly sliced green onion (optional)
  Fresh rosemary (optional)

● Rinse chicken; pat dry with paper towels. Cut chicken lengthwise into ½-inch-thick strips. On 2 long or 4 short skewers loosely thread chicken accordion-style. On 1 long or 2 short skewers, alternately thread the mushrooms and onions, and on 1 long or 2 short skewers, thread the sweet pepper pieces.

● In a small saucepan heat catsup and jelly. Brush over chicken and vegetables.

● Grill skewers on an uncovered grill directly over *medium* coals for 10 to 12 minutes or till the chicken is tender and no longer pink and the vegetables are crisp-tender, turning once and brushing with sauce. (Or, preheat broiler. Place skewers on unheated rack of a broiler pan. Broil 4 to 5 inches from heat for 12 to 14 minutes, turning once and brushing with sauce.) If desired, serve over hot rice with green onion and garnish with rosemary. Makes 4 servings.

Jalapeño Shrimp and Pasta

Keep fresh jalapeños on hand when you want to add spunk to a dish. To keep fresh peppers on hand for easy use, slice or chop them, then freeze them for up to 6 months. (See photograph pages 44 and 45.)

12	ounces fresh or frozen shrimp
1	fresh jalapeño pepper
1	tablespoon margarine or butter
1	medium onion, chopped
¼	teaspoon ground cumin
¼	teaspoon pepper
⅛	teaspoon salt
2	cloves garlic, minced
2	medium tomatoes, chopped (1⅓ cup)
1	4½-ounce can diced green chili peppers, drained
8	ounces penne, rigatoni, or cavatelli, cooked and drained

● Thaw shrimp, if frozen. Peel and devein shrimp. Halve any large shrimp. Wearing plastic gloves, seed and chop jalapeño pepper. In a 10-inch skillet heat margarine or butter over medium-high heat. Add shrimp, jalapeño pepper, onion, cumin, pepper, salt, and garlic. Cook, stirring frequently, for 1 to 3 minutes or till shrimp turn pink. Gently stir in tomato and chili peppers. Heat through. Serve immediately over hot cooked pasta. Makes 4 servings.

Too Hot to Handle

To protect yourself when working with hot peppers, cover your hands with plastic bags or plastic kitchen gloves. After you're done, discard the bags or gloves and be sure to wash your hands thoroughly before touching your eyes or face.

TOTAL FAT: 5 g
DAILY VALUE FAT: 8%
DAILY VALUE SATURATED FAT: 5%

NUTRITION FACTS PER SERVING:

Calories	345
Total Fat	5 g
Saturated Fat	1 g
Cholesterol	131 mg
Sodium	338 mg
Carbohydrate	51 g
Fiber	2 g
Protein	23 g

EXCHANGES:
1 Vegetable, 3 Starch, 1½ Meat

PREPARATION TIME: 15 minutes
COOKING TIME: 8 minutes

**NUTRITION FACTS
PER SERVING:**

Calories	340
Total Fat	6 g
Saturated Fat	1 g
Cholesterol	21 mg
Sodium	304 mg
Carbohydrate	56 g
Fiber	8 g
Protein	21 g

EXCHANGES:

2 Vegetable, 3 Starch, 1 Meat

PREPARATION TIME: 15 minutes
COOKING TIME: 17 minutes

Turkey-Mac Chili

Canned products often contain a lot of sodium. If your doctor has told you to watch your sodium intake, buy lower-sodium canned products, such as tomatoes or beans. Even if you add sodium at the table, you'll generally add less than what a regular sodium product contains.

Nonstick spray coating
8 **ounces lean ground raw turkey or**
  chicken
1 **medium onion, chopped (½ cup)**
2 **cloves garlic, minced**
1 **14½-ounce can low-sodium tomatoes,**
  cut up
1½ **cups water**
1 **15-ounce can low-sodium tomato sauce**
1 **cup elbow macaroni**
1 **tablespoon chili powder**
½ **teaspoon dried basil, crushed**
¼ **teaspoon pepper**
⅛ **teaspoon salt**
1 **15-ounce can low-sodium dark red**
  kidney beans, rinsed and drained
  Low-fat dairy sour cream or plain
  low-fat yogurt (optional)
  Ground red pepper (optional)
  Fresh cilantro (optional)

● Spray a large saucepan with nonstick coating. Cook the turkey or chicken, onion, and garlic in the saucepan till turkey or chicken is no longer pink and onion is tender. Stir in the *undrained* tomatoes, water, tomato sauce, *uncooked* macaroni, chili powder, basil, pepper, and salt. Bring to boiling. Reduce heat. Simmer, uncovered, for 17 to 20 minutes or till the pasta is tender and the mixture is of desired consistency. Stir in the beans; heat through.

● To serve, ladle chili into individual bowls. If desired, dollop with sour cream or yogurt, sprinkle with ground red pepper, and garnish with cilantro. Makes 4 servings.

TOTAL FAT: **7 g**
DAILY VALUE FAT: **11%**
DAILY VALUE SATURATED FAT: **10%**

**NUTRITION FACTS
PER SERVING:**

Calories	155
Total Fat	7 g
Saturated Fat	2 g
Cholesterol	32 mg
Sodium	233 mg
Carbohydrate	10 g
Fiber	0 g
Protein	13 g

EXCHANGES:
2 Meat, ½ Fruit

**PREPARATION TIME: 7 minutes
COOKING TIME: 10 minutes**

Turkey Patties with Chutney

You can purchase chutney, a sweet 'n' sour mixture, in a variety of flavors. Some of our favorites include mango, cranberry, pear, or apple chutney. If you like, serve these patties on toasted burger buns.

 1 **beaten egg white**
¼ **cup fine dry bread crumbs**
¼ **teaspoon salt**
¼ **teaspoon poultry seasoning or ground sage**
⅛ **teaspoon pepper**
12 **ounces lean ground raw turkey or chicken**
    Nonstick spray coating
 2 **tablespoons chutney, finely snipped**
⅛ **teaspoon ground ginger**

● In a medium mixing bowl stir together egg white, bread crumbs, salt, poultry seasoning or sage, and pepper. Add the ground turkey or chicken. Mix well. Shape the mixture into four ¾-inch thick patties.

● Spray the unheated rack of a broiler pan with nonstick coating. Place patties on rack. Broil 4 to 5 inches from the heat for 10 to 12 minute or till patties are no longer pink, turning once. Meanwhile stir together the chutney and ginger. To serve, spoon chutney mixture atop hot patties. Makes 4 servings.

Best-Bet Ground Poultry

Store-bought ground chicken and turkey often contain poultry skin, which has a high fat content. When buying ground poultry, choose a brand without the skin. If it's not available, ask your butcher to grind fresh chicken or turkey for you, or grind your own at home.

Turkey and Swiss Sandwiches

For a flavor twist, substitute smoked turkey breast for the turkey in these open-face sandwiches.

1 tablespoon nonfat mayonnaise dressing
or salad dressing
1 tablespoon Dijon-style mustard or spicy
brown mustard
4 slices rye or whole wheat bread
6 ounces sliced fully cooked turkey breast
2 plum tomatoes, thinly sliced
⅛ teaspoon pepper
2 ounces reduced-fat Swiss cheese, sliced

● In a small mixing bowl stir together the mayonnaise dressing or salad dressing and the Dijon-style or spicy brown mustard; set aside. Place bread slices on the unheated rack of a broiler pan. Broil 4 to 5 inches from the heat about 1 minute or till lightly toasted.

● Turn bread slices over. Spread mayonnaise mixture to the edges of untoasted sides of each slice. Top with turkey and tomato slices. Sprinkle with pepper. Top with Swiss cheese. Return to boiler. Broil for 1 to 2 minutes more or till heated through and cheese is melted. Makes 4 servings.

TOTAL FAT: 4 g
DAILY VALUE FAT: 6%
DAILY VALUE SATURATED FAT: 10%

NUTRITION FACTS PER SERVING:

Calories	182
Total Fat	4 g
Saturated Fat	2 g
Cholesterol	45 mg
Sodium	363 mg
Carbohydrate	15 g
Fiber	2 g
Protein	20 g

EXCHANGES:
1 Starch, 2½ Meat

PREPARATION TIME: 10 minutes
COOKING TIME: 3 minutes

Deli Meat Delights

Sliced turkey breast from the deli is a nutritional bargain when you compare it to other deli selections. Here's how it stacks up to an ounce of other lunchmeat favorites:

	Fat (grams)	Calories
Turkey breast	0.3	23
Beef salami	5	60
Beef bologna	7	72
Beef pastrami	8	99

TOTAL FAT: 11 g
DAILY VALUE FAT: 17%
DAILY VALUE SATURATED FAT: 10%

NUTRITION FACTS
PER SERVING:

Calories	237
Total Fat	11 g
Saturated Fat	2 g
Cholesterol	59 mg
Sodium	205 mg
Carbohydrate	10 g
Fiber	1 g
Protein	24 g

EXCHANGES:

½ Fruit, ½ Starch, 3 Meat

PREPARATION TIME: 25 minutes
COOKING TIME: 1 hour
STANDING TIME: 15 minutes

Apricot-Stuffed Grilled Turkey Breast

Here's a tip from our Test Kitchen: Use kitchen shears to snip the dried apricots. It's easier, faster, and less messy than a knife and cutting board.

1   2- to 2½-pound bone-in turkey breast half
1½ cups soft bread crumbs (2 slices)
½   cup snipped dried apricots
¼   cup chopped pecans, toasted
2   tablespoons apple juice or water
1   tablespoons cooking oil
¼   teaspoon dried rosemary, crushed
¼   teaspoon garlic salt
1   tablespoon Dijon-style mustard
1   tablespoon water

● Remove bone from turkey breast. Rinse turkey; pat dry with paper towels. Cut a horizontal slit into thickest part of turkey breast to form a 5x4-inch pocket. Set aside.

● In a medium mixing bowl, combine bread crumbs, apricots, pecans, apple juice or water, oil, rosemary, and garlic salt. Spoon stuffing mixture into pocket. Securely fasten the opening with water-soaked wooden toothpicks or tie with heavy cotton string. Stir together mustard and water; set aside.

● In a covered grill arrange preheated coals around a drip pan. Test for *medium* heat above pan. Place turkey on the grill rack directly over drip pan, not over the coals. Cover and grill about 1 hour or till turkey juices run clear (stuffing should reach 160°), brushing with mustard mixture during the last 15 minutes of cooking. Remove turkey from grill and cover with foil. Let stand for 15 minutes before slicing. Makes 8 servings.

TOTAL FAT: 3 g
DAILY VALUE FAT: 5%
DAILY VALUE SATURATED FAT: 5%

**NUTRITION FACTS
PER SERVING:**

Calories	372
Total Fat	3 g
Saturated Fat	1 g
Cholesterol	34 mg
Sodium	214 mg
Carbohydrate	59 g
Fiber	1 g
Protein	25 g

EXCHANGES:

1 Vegetable, 3½ Starch, 2 Meat

PREPARATION TIME: 10 minutes
COOKING TIME: 15 minutes

Sage and Cream Turkey Fettuccine

For a change, try pork tenderloin instead of the turkey. They are comparable in fat content. A 3-ounce portion of pork tenderloin has 4 grams of fat. A 3-ounce serving of turkey breast contains 3 grams of fat.

12 ounces turkey breast steak
 2 tablespoons all-purpose flour
 1 8-ounce carton fat-free dairy sour cream
 ½ cup reduced-sodium chicken broth
 ½ teaspoon dried sage, crushed
 ⅛ teaspoon pepper
    Nonstick spray coating
 ⅛ teaspoon salt
1½ cups sliced fresh mushrooms
 4 green onions, sliced (about ½ cup)
 1 clove garlic, minced
 8 ounces spinach fettuccine or plain
    fettuccine, cooked and drained

● Rinse turkey; pat dry with paper towels. Cut turkey steak into bite-size pieces. In a medium mixing bowl stir flour into sour cream. Stir in chicken broth, sage, and pepper. Set aside.

● Spray a large skillet with nonstick coating. Preheat the skillet over medium heat. Add turkey to skillet. Cook and stir turkey over medium heat for 4 to 5 minutes or till no longer pink. Sprinkle with salt. Remove turkey from skillet.

● Add mushrooms, green onion, and garlic to skillet. Cook and stir over medium heat about 3 minutes or till onion is tender. Return the turkey to the skillet. Stir sour cream mixture; add to the mixture in the skillet. Cook and stir over medium heat till thickened and bubbly. Cook and stir for 1 minute more. Serve over hot fettuccine. Makes 4 servings.

Creamy Chicken and Broccoli Soup

This creamy-tasting soup makes enough for 3 main dishes. If your family is larger, double the ingredients.

3 cups broccoli flowerets
1 14½-ounce can reduced-sodium chicken broth
2 tablespoons all-purpose flour
1 teaspoon snipped fresh basil or ¼ teaspoon dried basil, crushed
1 cup evaporated skim milk
1 cup chopped cooked chicken
Salt (optional)
Pepper (optional)

● In a medium saucepan combine the broccoli and ¾ *cup* of the broth. Bring to boiling. Reduce heat. Simmer, uncovered, for 8 to 12 minutes or till broccoli is tender.

● In a screw-top jar, combine the remaining chicken broth, the flour, and basil. Cover and shake to mix. Stir flour mixture into broth mixture in saucepan. Stir in milk. Cook and stir over medium-high heat till mixture is thickened and bubbly. Cook and stir for 1 minute more. Stir in chicken. Heat through. If desired, season to taste with salt and pepper. Makes 3 servings.

Worth Your Salt

The Dietary Guidelines recommend a daily limit of 2,400 mg of sodium. By making smart selections at the supermarket, you can keep your sodium intake in check. This comparison of chicken broth products illustrates the wide difference of sodium content available. Each is based on 1 cup of broth:

Low sodium broth	54 mg
Regular broth	776 mg
1 bouillon cube (makes 1 cup)	1,152 mg

TOTAL FAT: 5 g
DAILY VALUE FAT: 8%
DAILY VALUE SATURATED FAT: 5%

NUTRITION FACTS PER SERVING:

Calories	206
Total Fat	5 g
Saturated Fat	1 g
Cholesterol	48 mg
Sodium	514 mg
Carbohydrate	21 g
Fiber	2 g
Protein	27 g

EXCHANGES:
1 Milk, 2 Vegetable, 2 Meat

PREPARATION TIME: 10 minutes
COOKING TIME: 15 minutes

Skillet Chicken Paella

Paella, a Spanish rice dish, usually contains shellfish and other meats. This company-special chicken version takes just 30 minutes to prepare.

1¼ **pounds skinless, boneless chicken breasts**
  1 **tablespoon olive oil or cooking oil**
  1 **medium onion, chopped (½ cup)**
  2 **cloves garlic, minced**
2¼ **cups reduced-sodium chicken broth**
  1 **cup long grain rice**
  1 **teaspoon dried oregano, crushed**
  ½ **teaspoon paprika**
  ¼ **teaspoon salt**
  ¼ **teaspoon pepper**
  ⅛ **teaspoon ground saffron or ground
      turmeric**
  1 **14½-ounce can reduced-sodium
      stewed tomatoes**
  1 **medium red sweet pepper, cut into strips**
  ¾ **cup frozen peas**

● Rinse chicken; pat dry with paper towels. Cut chicken into bite-size strips. In a 10-inch skillet cook chicken strips, *half* at a time, in hot oil for 2 to 3 minutes or till no longer pink. Remove chicken from skillet. Set aside.

● Add onion and garlic to skillet; cook till tender but not brown. Add broth, *uncooked* rice, oregano, paprika, salt, pepper, and saffron or turmeric to skillet. Bring to boiling. Reduce heat. Simmer, covered, for 15 minutes.

● Add the *undrained* tomatoes, sweet pepper, and frozen peas to skillet. Cover and simmer about 5 minutes more or till rice is tender. Stir in cooked chicken. Cook and stir about 1 minute more or till heated through. Makes 6 servings.

TOTAL FAT: **6 g**
DAILY VALUE FAT: **9%**
DAILY VALUE SATURATED FAT: **5%**

NUTRITION FACTS
PER SERVING:

Calories	285
Total Fat	6 g
Saturated Fat	1 g
Cholesterol	50 mg
Sodium	415 mg
Carbohydrate	35 g
Fiber	3 g
Protein	23 g

EXCHANGES:

1 Vegetable, 2 Starch, 2 Meat

PREPARATION TIME: **10 minutes**
COOKING TIME: **25 minutes**

Curry Chicken and Fruit Salad

Select low-fat deli chicken or roast beef for this refreshing salad.

TOTAL FAT: **5 g**
DAILY VALUE FAT: **8%**
DAILY VALUE SATURATED FAT: **5%**

NUTRITION FACTS
PER SERVING:

Calories	233
Total Fat	5 g
Saturated Fat	1 g
Cholesterol	51 mg
Sodium	288 mg
Carbohydrate	28 g
Fiber	3 g
Protein	20 g

EXCHANGES:
1 Vegetable, 1½ Fruit, 2½ Meat

PREPARATION TIME: **20 minutes**

2 cups strawberry halves

1 11-ounce can pineapple tidbits and mandarin orange sections, drained (juice pack), or one 11-ounce can mandarin oranges sections, drained (water pack)

¼ cup nonfat mayonnaise dressing or salad dressing

¼ cup fat-free dairy sour cream

2 tablespoons frozen orange juice concentrate

¾ to 1 teaspoon curry powder

4 to 5 tablespoons skim milk

6 cups purchased torn mixed salad greens

8 ounces cooked chicken, cubed, or cooked roast beef, thinly sliced and rolled up

Toasted coconut (optional)

● In a medium mixing bowl toss together strawberries and drained canned fruit. Set aside.

● For dressing, in a small mixing bowl stir together the mayonnaise dressing or salad dressing, sour cream, orange juice concentrate, and curry powder. Stir in enough milk to make of drizzling consistency.

● Line 4 salad plates with torn mixed greens. Top with fruit mixture and cooked chicken or beef. Drizzle with the dressing. If desired, garnish with toasted coconut. Makes 4 servings.

Dilled Chicken and Potato Salad

No time to cook the chicken? Use chopped roasted chicken from the deli instead.

1 **pound whole tiny new potatoes,**
   quartered
12 **ounces skinless, boneless chicken breast**
   halves
1 **tablespoon olive oil or cooking oil**
1 **cup sliced celery**
1 **cup chopped green sweet pepper**
½ **cup nonfat Italian salad dressing**
2 **tablespoons snipped dill**
1 **tablespoon Dijon-style mustard**
2 **large tomatoes, halved and sliced**
1 **medium cucumber, thinly sliced**
   Fresh dill (optional)

● Cook potatoes, covered, in boiling salted water for 6 to 8 minutes or till tender; drain.

● Meanwhile, rinse chicken; pat dry. Cut into bite-size strips. In a large skillet cook chicken in hot oil over medium-high heat for 3 to 4 minutes till tender and no longer pink; remove chicken from skillet.

● In a large bowl place cooked potatoes, cooked chicken, celery, and green pepper. Toss gently. In a small bowl stir together salad dressing, snipped dill, and mustard. Drizzle over salad, tossing gently to coat.

● Arrange sliced tomatoes and cucumber on 4 dinner plates. Spoon salad over tomatoes and cucumber. If desired, garnish with fresh dill. Makes 4 servings.

TOTAL FAT: 7 g
DAILY VALUE FAT: 11%
DAILY VALUE SATURATED FAT: 5%

**NUTRITION FACTS
PER SERVING:**

Calories	283
Total Fat	7 g
Saturated Fat	1 g
Cholesterol	45 mg
Sodium	597 mg
Carbohydrate	36 g
Fiber	4 g
Protein	20 g

EXCHANGES:
1 Vegetable, 2 Starch, 2 Meat

PREPARATION TIME: 10 minutes
COOKING TIME: 10 minutes

Chicken with Lemon Mushroom Sauce

Pounding the chicken makes it tender and helps it cook lickity-split.

TOTAL FAT: **3 g**
DAILY VALUE FAT: **4%**
DAILY VALUE SATURATED FAT: **5%**

**NUTRITION FACTS
PER SERVING:**

Calories	110
Total Fat	3 g
Saturated Fat	1 g
Cholesterol	45 mg
Sodium	188 mg
Carbohydrate	4 g
Fiber	1 g
Protein	17 g

EXCHANGES:

1 Vegetable, 2 Meat

PREPARATION TIME: 10 minutes
COOKING TIME: 10 minutes

4   medium skinless, boneless chicken
    breast halves (12 ounces total)
⅛   teaspoon salt
⅛   teaspoon pepper
    Nonstick spray coating
½   cup reduced-sodium chicken broth
2   tablespoons lemon juice
1   tablespoon dry white wine (optional)
2   cups sliced fresh mushrooms
1   tablespoon water
2   teaspoons cornstarch
1   tablespoon snipped parsley
    Thin lemon slices (optional)

● Rinse chicken; pat dry with paper towels. Place each breast half, boned side up, between 2 pieces of clear plastic wrap. Working from the center to edges, pound lightly with the flat side of a mallet till ⅛ inch thick. Sprinkle chicken with salt and pepper.

● Spray a 12-inch skillet with nonstick coating. Preheat the skillet over medium heat. Cook chicken in hot skillet for 3 to 4 minutes or till no longer pink, turning once. Remove chicken from skillet. Place on a serving platter; cover with foil to keep warm.

● For sauce, in the same skillet stir together chicken broth, lemon juice, and, if desired, wine. Add mushrooms. Return to heat. Bring to boiling. Reduce heat. Simmer, covered, about 5 minutes or till mushrooms are done. Stir together water and cornstarch. Add to mixture in skillet. Bring to boiling. Cook and stir for 2 minutes more. Stir in parsley. Spoon over chicken. If desired, garnish with lemon slices. Makes 4 servings.

Jamaican Jerk Chicken

If you like, you can use 1 tablespoon purchased Jamaican Jerk seasoning in place of the crushed red pepper, salt, all-spice, curry powder, thyme, ginger, and black pepper.

4 **large skinless, boneless chicken breast halves (1 pound total)**
½ **cup coarsely chopped onion**
2 **tablespoons lime juice**
1 **teaspoon crushed red pepper**
½ **teaspoon salt**
½ **teaspoon ground allspice**
¼ **teaspoon curry powder**
⅛ **teaspoon dried thyme, crushed**
⅛ **teaspoon ground ginger**
¼ **teaspoon black pepper**
2 **cloves garlic, quartered**
1 **medium red, yellow, or green sweet pepper, cut into 1½-inch pieces**
1 **small zucchini, sliced ½-inch thick**
1 **tablespoon cooking oil**
¼ **teaspoon coarsely ground black pepper**

● Rinse chicken; pat dry with paper towels. In a blender container combine onion, lime juice, crushed red pepper, salt, allspice, curry powder, thyme, ginger, black pepper, and garlic. Cover and blend till smooth. Place chicken in a shallow dish. Add spice mixture; turn to coat both sides. Cover and chill for 30 minutes.

● Meanwhile, thread sweet pepper and zucchini pieces on four 8- to 10-inch skewers. Brush with oil and sprinkle with coarsely ground pepper. Remove chicken from spice mixture. Grill chicken on an uncovered grill directly over *medium* coals for 12 to 15 minutes or till tender and no longer pink, turning and brushing once with spice mixture. Add vegetables to grill during the last 10 minutes of cooking; turn frequently. Makes 4 servings.

TOTAL FAT: **7 g**
DAILY VALUE FAT: **11%**
DAILY VALUE SATURATED FAT: **5%**

NUTRITION FACTS PER SERVING:

Calories	176
Total Fat	7 g
Saturated Fat	1 g
Cholesterol	59 mg
Sodium	327 mg
Carbohydrate	6 g
Fiber	1 g
Protein	22 g

EXCHANGES:
1 Vegetable, 3 Meat

PREPARATION TIME: 15 minutes
CHILLING TIME: 30 minutes
COOKING TIME: 25 minutes

TOTAL FAT: **3 g**
DAILY VALUE FAT: **5%**
DAILY VALUE SATURATED FAT: **5%**

NUTRITION FACTS
PER SERVING:

Calories	146
Total Fat	3 g
Saturated Fat	1 g
Cholesterol	59 mg
Sodium	287 mg
Carbohydrate	6 g
Fiber	1 g
Protein	22 g

EXCHANGES:

½ Fruit, 3 Meat

PREPARATION TIME: **20 minutes**
MARINATING TIME: **30 minutes**
COOKING TIME: **12 minutes**

Chicken with Peach Salsa

If fresh peaches or papayas aren't in season, thaw and chop 1 cup frozen peach slices.

4 **large skinless, boneless chicken breast halves (1 pound total)**
2 **tablespoons lime juice**
4 **teaspoons teriyaki sauce or soy sauce**
1 **medium peach, peeled, pitted, and chopped, or ½ of a medium papaya, peeled, seeded, and chopped (about 1 cup)**
1 **small chopped tomato (½ cup)**
2 **tablespoons sliced green onion**
1 **tablespoon lime juice**
1 **teaspoon grated gingerroot or ¼ teaspoon ground ginger**
¼ **teaspoon bottled minced garlic or ⅛ teaspoon garlic powder**
   Hot cooked rice (optional)
   Fresh thyme (optional)

● Rinse chicken; pat dry with paper towels. In a small bowl stir together the 2 tablespoons lime juice and the teriyaki sauce or soy sauce. Brush chicken with the lime juice mixture. Cover and let stand at room temperature for 30 minutes or chill for up to 2 hours.

● For salsa, in a medium mixing bowl stir together peach or papaya, tomato, green onion, the 1 tablespoon lime juice, the gingerroot or ground ginger, and garlic or garlic powder. Cover and let stand at room temperature for 30 minutes or chill for up 2 hours.

● Place chicken on the unheated rack of a broiler pan. Broil 4 to 5 inches from the heat for 12 to 15 minutes or till no longer pink, turning once. If desired, serve chicken and salsa over hot cooked rice and garnish with thyme. Serve with salsa. Makes 4 servings.

Chicken-Olive Calzones

Calzones (KAHL-zones) are like a savory turnover. These calzones are stuffed with chicken, cheese, olives, and herbs. Dip them in warm purchased spaghetti sauce, if you like.

1½ **cups chopped cooked chicken (8 ounces)**
½ **cup shredded reduced-fat Monterey Jack cheese (2 ounces)**
¼ **cup chopped celery**
¼ **cup chopped pitted ripe olives**
½ **teaspoon dried basil, crushed**
¼ **teaspoon dried oregano, crushed**
⅛ **teaspoon garlic powder**
⅛ **teaspoon pepper**
⅓ **cup tub fat-free cream cheese**
Nonstick spray coating
1 **10-ounce package refrigerated pizza dough**
1 **beaten egg**
1 **tablespoon water**
Grated Parmesan cheese (optional)
Spaghetti sauce, heated (optional)

● For filling, in a medium bowl combine chicken, Monterey Jack cheese, celery, ripe olives, basil, oregano, garlic powder, and pepper. Stir in cream cheese. Set aside.

● Spray a baking sheet with nonstick coating; set aside. For calzones, unroll pizza dough. On a lightly floured surface roll the dough into a 15x10-inch rectangle. Cut into six 5-inch squares. Divide the chicken filling among the squares. Brush edges with *water*. Lift one corner and stretch dough over to the opposite corner. Seal edges of dough well with tines of a fork.

● Arrange calzones on the prepared baking sheet. Prick the tops with a fork. In a small bowl combine egg and 1 tablespoon water; brush over the calzones. If desired, sprinkle with the Parmesan cheese.

● Bake in a 425° oven for 10 to 12 minutes or till golden brown. Let stand for 5 minutes before serving. If desired, serve with warm spaghetti sauce. Makes 6 servings.

TOTAL FAT: 11 g
DAILY VALUE FAT: 17%
DAILY VALUE SATURATED FAT: 20%

**NUTRITION FACTS
PER SERVING:**

Calories	241
Total Fat	9 g
Saturated Fat	4 g
Cholesterol	81 mg
Sodium	315 mg
Carbohydrate	18 g
Fiber	1 g
Protein	18 g

EXCHANGES:
1 Starch, 2 Meat, ½ Fat

PREPARATION TIME: 15 minutes
COOKING TIME: 10 minutes
STANDING TIME: 5 minutes

TOTAL FAT: 4 g
DAILY VALUE FAT: 6%
DAILY VALUE SATURATED FAT: 5%

**NUTRITION FACTS
PER SERVING:**

Calories	166
Total Fat	4 g
Saturated Fat	1 g
Cholesterol	59 mg
Sodium	55 mg
Carbohydrate	11 g
Fiber	0 g
Protein	22 g

EXCHANGES:
1 Fruit, 1 Meat

PREPARATION TIME: 5 minutes
COOKING TIME: 10 minutes

Easy Orange-Glazed Chicken

Serve this flavorful chicken with wild rice and steamed fresh asparagus for a healthful meal.

 Nonstick spray coating
4 large skinless, boneless chicken breast
   halves (1 pound total)
 Several dashes paprika
½ of a 6-ounce can (⅓ cup) frozen orange
   juice concentrate, thawed
2 teaspoons snipped fresh rosemary or
   thyme or ½ teaspoon dried rosemary
   or thyme, crushed

● Rinse chicken; pat dry with paper towels. Lightly sprinkle with paprika. Spray a large nonstick skillet with nonstick coating. Cook chicken breast halves in skillet over medium heat about 4 minutes or till brown, turning once.

● Meanwhile, for glaze, stir together the orange juice concentrate and rosemary or thyme. Spoon over chicken breasts. Cover and cook over medium heat for 5 to 6 minutes more or till chicken is no longer pink. To serve, spoon glaze over chicken. Makes 4 servings.

Shedding the Skin

To cut down on fat, remove skin from poultry before you serve it. It's OK to leave the skin on during cooking because it adds flavor and keeps moistness in, yet the meat won't absorb much of the fat. For comparison, take a look at the difference between a 3.5-ounce serving of roasted chicken served with skin and without.

	Fat (grams)	Calories
Light meat with skin	10.9	222
Light meat without skin	4.5	173

Chicken Fingers with Honey Sauce

Serve your favorite barbecue sauce as a quick alternative to the honey sauce.

12 ounces skinless, boneless chicken breasts
2 beaten egg whites
1 tablespoon honey
2 cups cornflakes, crushed
¼ teaspoon pepper
¼ cup honey
4 teaspoons prepared mustard or
    Dijon-style mustard
¼ teaspoon garlic powder

● Rinse chicken; pat dry with paper towels. Cut chicken into ¾-inch wide, 3-inch long strips. In a small mixing bowl combine the egg whites and the 1 tablespoon honey. In a shallow bowl combine the cornflake crumbs and pepper. Dip chicken strips into the egg white mixture. Roll in the crumb mixture to coat. Place in a single layer on an ungreased baking sheet. Bake chicken in a 450° oven for 11 to 13 minutes or till no longer pink.

● Meanwhile, for sauce in a small bowl stir together the ¼ cup honey, mustard, and garlic powder. Serve with chicken. Makes 4 servings.

TOTAL FAT: 2 g
DAILY VALUE FAT: 3%
DAILY VALUE SATURATED FAT: 5%

NUTRITION FACTS PER SERVING:

Calories	230
Total Fat	2 g
Saturated Fat	1 g
Cholesterol	45 mg
Sodium	275 mg
Carbohydrate	31 g
Fiber	1 g
Protein	19 g

EXCHANGES:
2 Starch, 2½ Meat

PREPARATION TIME: 15 minutes
COOKING TIME: 11 minutes

TOTAL FAT: 7 g
DAILY VALUE FAT: 11%
DAILY VALUE SATURATED FAT: 10%

**NUTRITION FACTS
PER SERVING:**

Calories	157
Total Fat	7 g
Saturated Fat	2 g
Cholesterol	45 mg
Sodium	269 mg
Carbohydrate	10 g
Fiber	1 g
Protein	15 g

EXCHANGES:
2 Vegetable, 2 Meat

PREPARATION TIME: 15 minutes
COOKING TIME: 30 minutes

Spicy Hot Chicken Thighs

Pick your hotness level according to your taste buds' tolerance. Choose dried ancho or cascabel peppers for medium-hot, dried cayenne or pasilla peppers for hot, or dried pequin peppers for very hot.

2 fresh hot peppers, such as serrano or Thai, or 2 dried hot peppers
6 medium skinless, boneless chicken thighs (about 1¼ pounds total)
2 teaspoons cooking oil
1 medium onion, chopped (½ cup)
2 cloves garlic, minced
1 28-ounce can tomatoes, cut up
1 tablespoon brown sugar
1 teaspoon grated gingerroot

● Wearing plastic gloves, remove stem and seeds from hot peppers, if using. Cut into small pieces. Set aside.

● In a large skillet quickly brown chicken thighs on all sides in hot oil. Remove chicken from skillet. Cook onion and garlic in drippings in skillet till tender. Drain off fat, if necessary. Stir in chili peppers, *undrained* tomatoes, brown sugar, and gingerroot. Bring mixture to boiling.

● Return chicken thighs to skillet. Return to boiling. Reduce heat. Simmer, covered, for 20 to 30 minutes or till chicken is tender and no longer pink. Makes 6 servings.

Chicken with Basil and Beans

Beans add fiber and protein to your meals. This saucy dish has both butter beans and kidney beans.

2½ to 3 pounds meaty chicken pieces
   (breasts, thighs, and drumsticks),
   skinned
1 medium onion, chopped (½ cup)
1 clove garlic, minced
1 tablespoon cooking oil
1 14½-ounce can whole Italian-style
   tomatoes, cut up
1 tablespoon snipped fresh basil or
   1 teaspoon dried basil, crushed
1 tablespoon snipped fresh oregano or
   1 teaspoon dried oregano, crushed
½ teaspoon pepper
¼ teaspoon salt
1 15-ounce can butter beans, rinsed
   and drained
1 8-ounce can red kidney beans, rinsed and
   drained

● Rinse chicken; pat dry with paper towels. Set aside.

● In a 4½-quart Dutch oven cook onion and garlic in hot oil over medium heat till onion is tender. Add the *undrained* tomatoes, basil, oregano, pepper, and salt. Add chicken. Bring mixture to boiling. Reduce heat. Cover and simmer about 45 minutes or till chicken is tender and no longer pink.

● Transfer chicken to a serving platter; cover to keep warm. Stir butter beans and kidney beans into the Dutch oven; return to boiling. Simmer, uncovered, for 5 minutes more. Spoon bean mixture over chicken. Makes 6 servings.

TOTAL FAT: 8 g
DAILY VALUE FAT: 12%
DAILY VALUE SATURATED FAT: 10%

NUTRITION FACTS PER SERVING:

Calories	253
Total Fat	8 g
Saturated Fat	2 g
Cholesterol	61 mg
Sodium	468 mg
Carbohydrate	21 g
Fiber	7 g
Protein	27 g

EXCHANGES:
1½ Starch, 3 Meat

PREPARATION TIME: 15 minutes
COOKING TIME: 50 minutes

Ode to Beans

The humble bean deserves a place on everyone's plate. Unlike other high-protein sources, such as meat and cheese, beans contain almost no fat, no saturated fat, and no cholesterol. In addition, they're high in fiber. Kidney beans have about 8 grams fiber per ½-cup serving (about ⅓ of your minimum requirements for the day) and butter beans contain about 7 grams per ½ cup.

Hot 'n' Sweet Barbecued Chicken

Stir together just five ingredients for this finger-licking sauce.

TOTAL FAT: **8 g**
DAILY VALUE FAT: **12%**
DAILY VALUE SATURATED FAT: **10%**

NUTRITION FACTS
PER SERVING:

Calories	267
Total Fat	8 g
Saturated Fat	2 g
Cholesterol	92 mg
Sodium	353 mg
Carbohydrate	20 g
Fiber	1 g
Protein	30 g

EXCHANGES:

1½ Fruit, 4 Meat

PREPARATION TIME: **10 minutes**
COOKING TIME: **50 minutes**

¼ cup salsa
¼ cup catsup
¼ cup orange marmalade
1 tablespoon vinegar
½ teaspoon chili powder
½ teaspoon Worcestershire sauce
2 to 2½ pounds meaty chicken pieces (breasts, thighs, and drumsticks), skinned

● For sauce, in a small bowl stir together salsa, catsup, marmalade, vinegar, chili powder, and Worcestershire sauce.

● Rinse chicken; pat dry with paper towels. To grill, arrange *medium-hot* coals around a drip pan. Place chicken on grill rack directly over drip pan. Cover and grill for 50 to 60 minutes or till tender and no longer pink. Brush chicken generously with sauce during the last 10 minutes of grilling. (Or, to bake, arrange the chicken in a 2-quart-rectangular baking pan. Bake, uncovered, in a 375° oven for 30 minutes. Brush chicken generously with the sauce; bake for 10 to 15 minutes more or till tender and no longer pink.) Makes 4 servings.

TOTAL FAT: 11 g
DAILY VALUE FAT: 17%
DAILY VALUE SATURATED FAT: 10%

NUTRITION FACTS
PER SERVING:

Calories	370
Total Fat	11 g
Saturated Fat	2 g
Cholesterol	45 mg
Sodium	563 mg
Carbohydrate	48 g
Fiber	4 g
Protein	22 g

EXCHANGES:
½ Vegetable, 2½ Starch, 2 Meat,
½ Fruit, 1 Fat

SOAKING TIME: 30 minutes
PREPARATION TIME: 15 minutes
COOKING TIME: 7 minutes

Chicken and Apple Stir-Fry

You can use regular button mushrooms (about 2 cups sliced) instead of dried mushrooms in this dish. The dried wild mushrooms give the dish a more earthy flavor.

6 **dried wild mushrooms (1 cup), such as shiitake or wood ear mushrooms**
12 **ounces skinless, boneless chicken breast halves**
¾ **cup cold water**
3 **tablespoons frozen orange, apple, or pineapple juice concentrate, thawed**
2 **tablespoons soy sauce**
2 **teaspoons cornstarch**
¼ **teaspoon ground ginger**
¼ **teaspoon ground cinnamon**
⅛ **to ¼ teaspoon ground red pepper**
¼ **cup sliced or slivered almonds**
1 **tablespoon cooking oil**
2 **medium green, red, orange, and/or yellow sweet peppers, cut into thin 2-inch strips (2 cups)**
2 **medium apples, thinly sliced (2 cups)**
2 **cups hot cooked brown rice**

● In a small bowl cover mushrooms with warm water. Soak for 30 minutes. Rinse and squeeze mushrooms to drain. Discard stems. Thinly slice caps. Set aside.

● Meanwhile, rinse chicken; pat dry with paper towels. Cut chicken into 1-inch pieces. Set aside.

● For sauce, in a small bowl stir together cold water, juice concentrate, soy sauce, cornstarch, ginger, cinnamon, and red pepper. Set aside.

● Preheat a wok or large skillet over medium-high heat. Add almonds; stir-fry for 2 to 3 minutes or till golden. Remove almonds from the wok. Let the wok or skillet cool. Pour cooking oil into the wok or large skillet. (Add more oil as necessary during cooking.) Add the drained mushrooms, sweet peppers, and apples; stir-fry for 1 to 2 minutes or till peppers and apples are crisp-tender. Remove apple mixture from wok.

● Add chicken to hot wok; stir-fry for 3 to 4 minutes or till no longer pink. Push chicken from center of wok. Stir sauce; add to center of wok. Cook and stir till thickened and bubbly. Return apple mixture to wok. Stir all ingredients together to coat with sauce. Cook and stir for 1 to 2 minutes more or till heated through. Stir in the almonds. Serve immediately over hot cooked brown rice. Makes 4 servings.

TOTAL FAT: **7 g**
DAILY VALUE FAT: **11%**
DAILY VALUE SATURATED FAT: **5%**

**NUTRITION FACTS
PER SERVING:**

Calories	242
Total Fat	8 g
Saturated Fat	1 g
Cholesterol	73 mg
Sodium	237 mg
Carbohydrate	11 g
Fiber	0 g
Protein	29 g

EXCHANGES:

1 Starch, 3½ Meat

**PREPARATION TIME: 10 minutes
COOKING TIME: 45 minutes**

Oven-Fried Chicken

For the cracker coating, place the crackers in a plastic bag and use a rolling pin to crush them.

⅔ cup crushed low-fat crackers or
    crushed onion-flavored crackers
    (about 40 crackers)
¼ teaspoon ground red pepper
4 medium chicken breasts (1½ pounds
    total), skinned
1 slightly beaten egg white
1 tablespoon water
1 tablespoon margarine or butter, melted

● Place crushed crackers in a pie plate. Stir in the red pepper. Set aside.

● Rinse chicken; pat dry with paper towels. Combine the egg white and water. Brush chicken with egg mixture. Sprinkle crumb mixture over the chicken; gently press crumbs onto the chicken. Place chicken in an ungreased shallow baking pan. Drizzle with the melted margarine or butter.

● Bake in a 375° oven for 45 to 55 minutes or till tender and no longer pink. Transfer chicken to a serving platter. Makes 4 servings.

Taco Salad

Canned beans that have no salt added will save about 160 milligrams sodium per serving.

Nonstick spray coating
12 ounces lean ground raw turkey or
    chicken
1   15½-ounce can dark red kidney beans,
    rinsed and drained
1   14½-ounce can low-sodium tomatoes,
    cut up
1   4½-ounce can diced green chili peppers,
    drained
1   tablespoon chili powder
½   teaspoon ground cumin
4   cups purchased torn mixed salad greens
½   cup shredded reduced-fat cheddar cheese
    (2 ounces)
¼   cup fat-free dairy sour cream or plain
    fat-free yogurt
    Baked tortilla chips (optional)

● Spray a large skillet with nonstick coating. Cook the turkey or chicken in the skillet over medium heat about 5 minutes or till no longer pink. Drain off any fat. Stir in kidney beans, *undrained* tomatoes, chili peppers, chili powder, and cumin. Bring to boiling. Reduce heat. Simmer, covered, for 3 minutes. Uncover. Return to boiling. Reduce heat. Simmer, uncovered, for 5 to 10 minutes or to desired consistency.

● Meanwhile, arrange salad greens on 4 serving plates. Top each with some of the hot turkey or chicken mixture. Sprinkle with cheese. Dollop with sour cream or yogurt. If desired, serve with tortilla chips. Makes 4 servings.

TOTAL FAT: 11 g
DAILY VALUE FAT: 17%
DAILY VALUE SATURATED FAT: 15%

**NUTRITION FACTS
PER SERVING:**

Calories	291
Total Fat	11 g
Saturated Fat	3 g
Cholesterol	42 mg
Sodium	439 mg
Carbohydrate	28 g
Fiber	8 g
Protein	26 g

EXCHANGES:
2 Vegetable, 1 Starch, 3 Meat

PREPARATION TIME: 10 minutes
COOKING TIME: 15 minutes

Peppered Steak with Mushroom Sauce

Tenderloin is one of the leanest cuts of beef. To keep the steaks at their moist and juicy best, don't overcook them.

6 beef tenderloin steaks or 3 beef top loin
  steaks, cut 1 inch thick (about
  1½ pounds total)
1½ teaspoons dried whole green
  peppercorns, crushed, or ½ teaspoon
  coarsely ground black pepper
½ teaspoon dried thyme, crushed
½ teaspoon dried oregano, crushed
¼ teaspoon salt
  Nonstick spray coating
⅓ cup water
½ teaspoon instant beef bouillon granules
¾ cup sliced fresh shiitake mushrooms or
  other fresh mushrooms
¾ cup skim milk
2 tablespoons all-purpose flour
½ teaspoon dried thyme, crushed
⅔ cup fat-free or light dairy sour cream
1 tablespoon snipped chives
  (optional)

● Trim any fat from the meat. Combine the peppercorns or pepper, the first ½ teaspoon thyme, the oregano, and salt. Sprinkle each side of steaks with the mixture, pressing into meat.

● Spray a cold large nonstick skillet with nonstick spray coating. Preheat skillet. Add steaks to the skillet and cook over medium heat for 6 minutes. Turn and cook for 5 to 6 minutes more for medium doneness. Remove meat from skillet. Cover and keep warm.

● Add water and bouillon granules to skillet. Bring to boiling. Add mushrooms. Cook about 2 minutes or till tender. Stir together milk, flour, and the ½ teaspoon thyme. Add to skillet. Cook and stir till thickened and bubbly. Stir in sour cream; heat through, but *do not boil*. To serve, spoon sauce over steaks. If desired, garnish with chives. Makes 6 servings.

TOTAL FAT: 7 g
DAILY VALUE FAT: 11%
DAILY VALUE SATURATED FAT: 15%

**NUTRITION FACTS
PER SERVING:**

Calories	206
Total Fat	7 g
Saturated Fat	3 g
Cholesterol	64 mg
Sodium	243 mg
Carbohydrate	9 g
Fiber	0 g
Protein	25 g

EXCHANGES:
½ Milk, 3 Meat

PREPARATION TIME: 10 minutes
COOKING TIME: 20 minutes

TOTAL FAT: **12 g**
DAILY VALUE FAT: **18%**
DAILY VALUE SATURATED FAT: **20%**

NUTRITION FACTS
PER SERVING:

Calories	388
Total Fat	12 g
Saturated Fat	4 g
Cholesterol	43 mg
Sodium	541 mg
Carbohydrate	45 g
Fiber	1 g
Protein	24 g

EXCHANGES:

1 Vegetable, 2½ Starch, 2 Meat,
1 Fat

PREPARATION TIME: **15 minutes**
MARINATING TIME: **4 hours**
COOKING TIME: **15 minutes**

Marinated Steak Fajitas

*Fajitas are the rage in Mexican restaurants but you can easily make them at home. Top them with
fat-free dairy sour cream, chopped tomato, and fresh cilantro, if you like.*

3 tablespoons chili sauce
2 tablespoons water
1 tablespoon Worcestershire sauce
1 teaspoon dried oregano, crushed
½ teaspoon chili powder
⅛ teaspoon garlic powder
⅛ teaspoon pepper
1 pound beef flank steak
10 7-inch flour tortillas
Nonstick spray coating
2 small red, yellow, or green sweet peppers,
cut into thin bite-size strips
1 small onion, cut into thin wedges

● For marinade, in a small mixing bowl stir
together chili sauce, water, Worcestershire sauce,
oregano, chili powder, garlic powder, and pepper.
Trim any fat from meat. Cut meat, across
the grain, into thin bite-size strips. Place meat
in a plastic bag set in a shallow dish. Pour
marinade over meat. Close bag. Marinate in
the refrigerator for 4 to 24 hours, turning
occasionally.

● Wrap tortillas in foil and bake in a 350° oven
about 10 minutes or till warm. [Or, just before
serving, micro-cook tortillas, covered, on 100%
power (high) about 1 minute or till warm.]

● Spray a large nonstick skillet with nonstick
spray. Preheat over medium-high heat. Add *half*
of the meat mixture to the hot skillet. Cook and
stir for 3 to 4 minutes or to desired doneness.
Remove meat from the skillet. Repeat with the
remaining meat mixture (add 1 teaspoon
cooking oil, if necessary). Remove meat from
the skillet, reserving juices in skillet.

● Add pepper strips and onion wedges to juices
in skillet. Bring to boiling. Reduce heat. Simmer,
covered, for 3 to 4 minutes or till vegetables are
crisp-tender. Stir meat into vegetables in skillet.
Heat through. To serve, place *½ cup* of the meat-
vegetable mixture on each tortilla. Roll up.
Makes 5 servings.

Zesty Flank Steak with Corn Relish

Marinate flank steak several hours ahead or overnight so it's full of flavor by broiling time. Also, make the salsa ahead of time to blend the flavors.

1   8¾-ounce can whole kernel corn, drained
¾   cup green or regular salsa
1   medium tomato, chopped (about ⅔ cup)
¾   cup nonfat Italian salad dressing
2   tablespoons cracked black pepper
1   tablespoon Worcestershire sauce
1   teaspoon ground cumin
1¼ to 1½ pounds beef flank steak
    Fresh cilantro (optional)

● In a storage container combine corn, salsa, and tomato. Chill, covered, for up to 2 days. (Bring to room temperature before serving.)

● For marinade, in a bowl combine salad dressing, pepper, Worcestershire sauce, and cumin.

● With a knife, score steak at 1-inch intervals in a diamond pattern on both sides. Place meat in a large plastic bag set in a shallow dish. Pour marinade over meat. Close bag; marinate in refrigerator for 6 to 24 hours, turning bag once.

● To cook, drain the steak and discard the marinade. Place the steak on the unheated rack of a broiler pan. Broil 3 inches from heat for 12 to 15 minutes or to desired doneness, turning steak over after half of the broiling time. Slice the steak diagonally across the grain into very thin slices. Spoon corn salsa over meat. If desired, garnish with cilantro. Makes 6 servings.

TOTAL FAT: 10 g
DAILY VALUE FAT: 15%
DAILY VALUE SATURATED FAT: 10%

NUTRITION FACTS PER SERVING:

Calories	197
Total Fat	10 g
Saturated Fat	2 g
Cholesterol	44 mg
Sodium	313 mg
Carbohydrate	9 g
Fiber	2 g
Protein	19 g

EXCHANGES:

2 Vegetable, 2½ Meat

PREPARATION TIME: 15 minutes
MARINATING TIME: 6 hours
COOKING TIME: 12 minutes

TOTAL FAT: 8 g
DAILY VALUE FAT: 12%
DAILY VALUE SATURATED FAT: 10%

**NUTRITION FACTS
PER SERVING:**

Calories	153
Total Fat	8 g
Saturated Fat	2 g
Cholesterol	27 mg
Sodium	114 mg
Carbohydrate	8 g
Fiber	2 g
Protein	13 g

EXCHANGES:

1½ Vegetable, 1½ Meat

PREPARATION TIME: 25 minutes
MARINATING TIME: 4 hours
COOKING TIME: 2 minutes

Beef and Basil Salad

When you cook with lively-tasting ingredients, you don't have to rely on adding a lot of fat or sodium for flavor. Fresh herbs, spices, and vinegar are three such flavor boosters.

1 large tomato, chopped (1 cup)
½ of a yellow sweet pepper, cut into thin strips (½ cup)
¼ cup snipped basil
2 tablespoons balsamic vinegar
1 tablespoon olive oil
1 clove garlic, minced
8 ounces beef flank steak or lean beef top loin steak
6 cups torn mixed greens
Nonstick spray coating
1 clove garlic, minced
¼ teaspoon black pepper
⅛ teaspoon salt

● In a medium mixing bowl stir together the tomato, sweet pepper, and basil. In a screw-top jar combine vinegar, olive oil, and the clove garlic. Cover and shake to mix. Pour over vegetable mixture, tossing to coat. Cover and refrigerate for 4 to 24 hours.

● Meanwhile, partially freeze beef. Trim any fat from meat. Cut into thin bite-size strips. Arrange mixed greens on 4 salad plates.

● Spray a large skillet with nonstick coating. Add beef and the clove garlic. Cook and stir over medium-high heat for 2 to 3 minutes or to desired doneness. Sprinkle with pepper and salt. Stir in tomato mixture. Heat through. Top each salad with some of the hot beef-vegetable mixture. Serve immediately. Makes 4 servings.

Never-Too-Thin Beef

To slice beef ever-so-thinly, freeze the meat for about 45 to 60 minutes before you cut it. Then, using a sharp knife, cut the frozen meat against the grain into ¼-inch-thick slices.

TOTAL FAT: **5 g**
DAILY VALUE FAT: **8%**
DAILY VALUE SATURATED FAT: **10%**

NUTRITION FACTS
PER SERVING:

Calories	165
Total Fat	5 g
Saturated Fat	2 g
Cholesterol	59 mg
Sodium	68 mg
Carbohydrate	3 g
Fiber	1 g
Protein	25 g

EXCHANGES:
3½ Meat

PREPARATION TIME: **10 minutes**
COOKING TIME: **1¼ hours**

Spice-Rubbed Roast

This herb-and-spice combination does double duty. It's used as a rub for the meat and to season the sauce.

1 **2- to 2½-pound beef eye of round roast**
1 **tablespoon chili powder**
1½ **teaspoons ground cumin**
½ **teaspoon dried oregano, crushed**
¼ **teaspoon garlic powder**
⅛ **teaspoon ground red pepper**
    Nonstick spray coating
1 **small onion, chopped (⅓ cup)**
½ **of a 14½-ounce can low-sodium**
    tomatoes, cut up

● Trim any fat from meat. In a small mixing bowl stir together the chili powder, cumin, oregano, garlic powder, and red pepper. Sprinkle *2 teaspoons* of the spice mixture over meat; rub spice mixture into roast.

● Place roast on a rack in a shallow roasting pan. Insert a meat thermometer into roast. Roast in a 325° oven for 1¼ to 1¾ hours for medium-rare (145°) or for 1¾ to 2¼ hours for medium (155°). Remove meat from pan. Cover; let stand 15 minutes before carving. (Meat temperature will rise 5° during standing.)

● Meanwhile, for sauce, spray a small saucepan with nonstick coating. Cook onion in saucepan over medium heat for 2 to 3 minutes or till tender. Stir in *undrained* tomatoes and remaining spice mixture. Bring to boiling. Reduce heat. Simmer, uncovered, for 10 to 15 minutes or to desired consistency. To serve, thinly slice meat. Pass sauce with meat. Makes 8 to 10 servings.

Stir-Fried Beef and Apple Salad

For a splash of citrus, try substituting sectioned oranges for the apple.

¼ cup rice vinegar
1 tablespoon salad oil
2 teaspoons reduced-sodium soy sauce
2 teaspoons snipped chives
1 teaspoon honey or brown sugar
¼ teaspoon ground cinnamon
  Dash salt
8 ounces beef top round steak
  Nonstick spray coating
1 teaspoon toasted sesame oil
½ teaspoon coarsely cracked pepper
6 cups purchased torn mixed salad greens
1 medium red apple, cored and thinly sliced

● For dressing, in a screw-top jar combine rice vinegar, salad oil, soy sauce, chives, honey or brown sugar, cinnamon, and salt. Cover and shake to mix well. Set aside.

● Trim any fat from meat. Thinly slice beef into bite-size strips. Spray a large skillet with nonstick coating. Add sesame oil to the skillet. Preheat over medium-high heat. Add the beef. Stir-fry for 2 to 3 minutes or to desired doneness. Sprinkle meat with pepper.

● To serve, place mixed greens on 4 serving plates. Arrange apple slices and meat atop greens. Shake dressing. Drizzle each salad with some of the dressing. Makes 4 servings.

Red Meat Matters

Q. Is it OK to have beef on a low-fat diet?

A. Yes, as long as you choose lean cuts. Thanks to new breeding and feeding techniques, such cuts are more readily available today. Butchers are doing their part, too, by trimming visible fat more closely. As a result, calories, fat, and cholesterol have all been slashed.

Choose the following for the leanest cuts:

Bottom round roast
Top round steak or roast
Eye round roast
Arm pot roast

Round tip roast
T-bone steak
Top loin steak
Sirloin steak

TOTAL FAT: 8 g
DAILY VALUE FAT: 12%
DAILY VALUE SATURATED FAT: 10%

NUTRITION FACTS PER SERVING:

Calories	159
Total Fat	8 g
Saturated Fat	2 g
Cholesterol	36 mg
Sodium	155 mg
Carbohydrate	9 g
Fiber	2 g
Protein	15 g

EXCHANGES:
2 Vegetable, 1½ Meat

PREPARATION TIME: 15 minutes
COOKING TIME: 2 minutes

Spicy Beef and Bean Burgers

Using beans to replace some of the ground meat in recipes has many nutritional benefits.
They add protein, carbohydrates, and fiber without adding fat or cholesterol.

1 slightly beaten egg white
½ of a 15-ounce can (¾ cup) pinto beans,
    drained and mashed
¼ cup soft whole wheat bread crumbs
¼ cup finely chopped celery
1 tablespoon canned diced green chili
    peppers or 1 teaspoon chopped
    canned jalapeño peppers
⅛ teaspoon garlic powder
1 pound lean ground beef
4 7-inch flour tortillas, halved
8 lettuce leaves
1 cup salsa

● In a large mixing bowl combine egg white, beans, bread crumbs, celery, chili peppers, and garlic powder. Add ground beef; mix well.

● Shape meat mixture into eight ½-inch-thick oval patties. Place the patties on the unheated rack of a broiler pan. Broil 4 inches from the heat for 12 to 14 minutes or till the juices run clear, turning once.

● To serve, place a lettuce leaf and a burger in the center of each tortilla half. Top burger with *1 tablespoon* of the salsa. Bring ends of tortilla up and over burger. Top with another tablespoon salsa. Makes 8 servings.

TOTAL FAT: 8 g
DAILY VALUE FAT: 12%
DAILY VALUE SATURATED FAT: 10%

NUTRITION FACTS PER SERVING:

Calories	185
Total Fat	8 g
Saturated Fat	2 g
Cholesterol	36 mg
Sodium	339 mg
Carbohydrate	16 g
Fiber	2 g
Protein	14 g

EXCHANGES:
1 Starch, 2 Meat

PREPARATION TIME: 15 minutes
COOKING TIME: 12 minutes

TOTAL FAT: 3 g
DAILY VALUE FAT: 5%
DAILY VALUE SATURATED FAT: 5%

NUTRITION FACTS
PER SERVING:

Calories	199
Total Fat	3 g
Saturated Fat	1 g
Cholesterol	60 mg
Sodium	147 mg
Carbohydrate	23 g
Fiber	2 g
Protein	20 g

EXCHANGES:

1½ Fruit, 3 Meat

PREPARATION TIME: 25 minutes
COOKING TIME: 25 minutes

Fruit-Stuffed Pork Roast

Pork tenderloin fits nicely into a healthful diet because it is very lean, with only 4 grams of fat per 3-ounce serving.

½ cup mixed dried fruit bits
 2 tablespoon orange juice or apple juice
¼ cup unsweetened applesauce
12 ounces pork tenderloin
¼ teaspoon dried rosemary, crushed
⅛ teaspoon dried sage, crushed
⅛ teaspoon pepper
⅓ cup soft whole wheat or pumpernickel
     bread crumbs (½ slice)
¼ teaspoon lemon-pepper seasoning
 1 cup unsweetened applesauce
⅛ teaspoon ground nutmeg or cinnamon
     Fresh rosemary or sage sprigs (optional)
     Apple slices (optional)

● In a small mixing bowl combine the dried fruit bits, orange or apple juice, and the ¼ cup applesauce. Let stand at room temperature while preparing roast.

● Trim any fat from meat. Using a sharp knife, make a lengthwise cut down the center of the roast, cutting to, but not through, the other side. Spread the roast flat. Place between 2 sheets of plastic wrap and pound with the flat side of a meat mallet to ⅜-inch thickness.

● For stuffing, stir rosemary, sage, and pepper into fruit mixture. Stir in the bread crumbs. Spread the stuffing on the meat. Roll up jelly-roll style. Tie meat with string, first at center, then at 1-inch intervals.

● Place meat on a rack in a shallow roasting pan. Sprinkle lightly with lemon-pepper seasoning. Insert a meat thermometer. Roast in a 425° oven for 25 to 35 minutes or till thermometer registers 160°. Remove meat from pan. Cover with foil and let stand 5 to 10 minutes before carving.

● Meanwhile, in a small saucepan cook and stir the 1 cup applesauce and nutmeg or cinnamon over medium heat for 3 to 5 minutes or just till warm. To serve, remove strings from roast and thinly slice. If desired, garnish with additional fresh herb or apple slices. Serve with warm applesauce. Makes 4 servings.

Spicy Pork Chops

Vegetable juice cocktail is the base for this zippy tomato marinade. Try the hot-style version, which will give you extra heat.

4 **boneless pork loin chops, cut ½-inch thick (1¼ pound total)**
1 **6-ounce can (¾ cup) vegetable juice cocktail**
2 **tablespoons sliced green onion**
2 **tablespoons canned diced green chili peppers**
1 **clove garlic, minced**
1 **teaspoon Worcestershire sauce**
½ **teaspoon dried basil, crushed**
  Few dashes bottled hot pepper sauce
2 **cups hot cooked orzo or rice**

● Trim any fat from pork chops. Combine the vegetable juice cocktail, green onion, chili peppers, garlic, Worcestershire sauce, basil, and hot pepper sauce.

● Place chops in a plastic bag set in a shallow bowl. Pour juice mixture over meat. Close bag and turn to coat. Chill for 2 to 24 hours, turning the bag occasionally.

● Drain chops, reserving marinade. Place chops on the unheated rack of a broiler pan. Broil 3 to 4 inches from the heat for 4 minutes. Turn; broil for 4 to 5 minutes more or till slightly pink and juices run clear. In a small saucepan heat reserved marinade to a full boil. Serve the hot marinade with the pork chops and hot orzo or rice. Makes 4 servings.

A Leaner Pork Chop

Q. Can pork have a place in a healthful diet?

A. Of course. Today's pork comes from a leaner hog, and its visible fat is more closely trimmed. A 3-ounce portion of a pork loin chop (trimmed of fat) has about 170 calories and 7 grams of fat.

TOTAL FAT: 11 g
DAILY VALUE FAT: 17%
DAILY VALUE SATURATED FAT: 20%

NUTRITION FACTS PER SERVING:

Calories	273
Total Fat	11 g
Saturated Fat	4 g
Cholesterol	63 mg
Sodium	241 mg
Carbohydrate	21 g
Fiber	1 g
Protein	22 g

EXCHANGES:
3 Meat, 1 Starch, ½ Vegetable

PREPARATION TIME: 10 minutes
CHILLING TIME: 2 hours
COOKING TIME: 8 minutes

Barbecued Pork Sandwiches

Making your own barbecue sauce, rather than using a commercial sauce, reduces the sodium content in this recipe by almost half.

Nonstick spray coating
2 **cloves garlic, minced**
1 **medium onion, chopped (½ cup)**
½ **cup water**
½ **of a 6-ounce can (⅓ cup) tomato paste**
¼ **cup red wine vinegar**
1 **tablespoon brown sugar**
1½ **teaspoons chili powder**
1 **teaspoon dried oregano, crushed**
1 **teaspoon Worcestershire sauce**
12 **ounces pork tenderloin**
1 **medium green sweet pepper, chopped (¾ cup)**
4 **whole wheat buns, split and toasted**

● For sauce, spray a small saucepan with nonstick coating. Cook garlic and onion in the saucepan till tender. Stir in water, tomato paste, vinegar, brown sugar, chili powder, oregano, and Worcestershire sauce. Bring to boiling. Reduce heat. Simmer, uncovered, about 20 minutes or till desired consistency, stirring occasionally.

● Meanwhile, trim any fat from meat. Cut into bite-size strips. Spray a large skillet with nonstick coating. Add pork to skillet. Cook and stir pork over medium-high heat for 2 to 3 minutes or till juices run clear. Stir in green pepper and sauce. Heat through. Spoon mixture onto bottoms of buns. Cover with bun tops. Makes 4 servings.

TOTAL FAT: 5 g
DAILY VALUE FAT: 8%
DAILY VALUE SATURATED FAT: 10%

NUTRITION FACTS PER SERVING:

Calories	255
Total Fat	5 g
Saturated Fat	2 g
Cholesterol	60 mg
Sodium	305 mg
Carbohydrate	30 g
Fiber	2 g
Protein	24 g

EXCHANGES:
2½ Meat, 2 Starch

PREPARATION TIME: 20 minutes
COOKING TIME: 20 minutes

Pork with Cranberry-Pepper Relish

Serve any leftover relish with grilled turkey or beef steaks.

TOTAL FAT: **4 g**
DAILY VALUE FAT: **6%**
DAILY VALUE SATURATED FAT: **5%**

NUTRITION FACTS
PER SERVING WITH 2 TABLE-
SPOONS RELISH:

Calories	244
Total Fat	4 g
Saturated Fat	1 g
Cholesterol	60 mg
Sodium	73 mg
Carbohydrate	29 g
Fiber	0 g
Protein	19 g

EXCHANGES:
2 Fruit, 2½ Meat

PREPARATION TIME: **10 minutes**
COOKING TIME: **6 minutes**

12 ounces pork tenderloin
1 teaspoon cooking oil
¼ cup sliced green onion
1 10-ounce package frozen cranberry-
   orange relish, thawed
2 to 3 teaspoons bottled chopped green
   jalapeño peppers

● Trim any fat from meat. Cut meat into ½-inch thick slices. In a 10-inch nonstick skillet cook meat in hot oil over medium heat for 4 to 6 minutes or till no longer pink, turning once. Remove from skillet. Keep warm.

● Add green onion to skillet. Cook and stir till tender. Stir in cranberry-orange relish and jalapeño peppers. Cook and stir till heated through. To serve, place pork slices on 4 serving plates. Top each serving with *2 tablespoons* of the relish mixture. (Cover and chill any remaining relish mixture for up to 3 days.) Makes 4 servings.

Pork Chops with Apples

This tasty combination is brought up to date in this savory low-fat version.

4 pork loin chops, cut ½-inch thick
    (about 1¼ pounds total)
½ teaspoon dried sage, crushed
    Nonstick spray coating
1 small onion, sliced and separated into
    rings
2 medium apples, cored and cut into thin
    wedges
1 cup apple cider or apple juice
1 teaspoon brown sugar
1 tablespoon cold water
2 teaspoons cornstarch
2 cups hot cooked brown rice

● Trim any fat from chops. Rub sage onto both sides of the chops.

● Spray a cold 12-inch skillet with nonstick coating. Preheat skillet. Cook the chops for 5 minutes. Turn chops and add onion. Cook for 5 to 7 minutes more or till no pink remains. Remove chops and onion from skillet; keep chops warm. Wipe out skillet with paper towels.

● For the sauce, in the same skillet stir together the apple wedges, cider or juice, and brown sugar. Bring to boiling; reduce heat. Simmer, covered, for 3 to 5 minutes or till apples are crisp-tender.

● Combine water and cornstarch. Add to skillet mixture. Cook and stir thickened and bubbly. Cook and stir for 2 minutes more. Serve pork chops and apple mixture with hot brown rice. Makes 4 servings.

TOTAL FAT: 12 g
DAILY VALUE FAT: 18%
DAILY VALUE SATURATED FAT: 20%

NUTRITION FACTS PER SERVING:

Calories	357
Total Fat	12 g
Saturated Fat	4 g
Cholesterol	63 mg
Sodium	56 mg
Carbohydrate	43 g
Fiber	3 g
Protein	21 g

EXCHANGES:
2 Fruit, 3 Meat, 1 Starch

PREPARATION TIME: 10 minutes
COOKING TIME: 20 minutes

TOTAL FAT: 4 g
DAILY VALUE FAT: 6%
DAILY VALUE SATURATED FAT: 5%

**NUTRITION FACTS
PER SERVING:**

Calories	240
Total Fat	4 g
Saturated Fat	1 g
Cholesterol	60 mg
Sodium	334 mg
Carbohydrate	32 g
Fiber	3 g
Protein	21 g

EXCHANGES:

½ Vegetable, 2 Fruit, 3 Meat

PREPARATION TIME: 10 minutes
COOKING TIME: 25 minutes

Mustard-Orange Pork Tenderloin

A mixture of vegetables, such as small red onions, baby carrots, and chunks of zucchini, can be roasted alongside the meat. See directions for roasting them below.

> 12 **ounces pork tenderloin**
> ½ **cup apricot preserves or orange marmalade**
> 3 **tablespoons Dijon-style mustard**
> **Nonstick spray coating**
> 2 **cups sliced fresh mushrooms**
> ½ **cup sliced green onion**
> 2 **tablespoons orange juice**

● Trim any fat from meat. Place in a shallow roasting pan. Insert a meat thermometer. Roast, uncovered, in a 425° oven for 10 minutes.

● Meanwhile in a small mixing bowl stir together preserves and mustard. Spoon *half* of the mustard mixture over the tenderloin; set remaining mixture aside. Roast for 15 to 25 minutes more or till thermometer registers 160°. Cover meat with foil and let stand for 5 minutes before carving.

● Spray a medium saucepan with nonstick coating. Add mushrooms and onion. Cook and stir for 2 to 3 minutes or till mushrooms are tender. Stir in remaining mustard mixture and orange juice. Cook and stir till heated through. To serve, thinly slice roast. Spoon mushroom mixture over roast. Makes 4 servings.

Nutrition-Packed Vegetables

Vegetables should be an important part of any low-fat eating plan. They're low-fat nutrition dynamos, rich in vitamin C, beta carotene, and fiber. You should strive to eat at least three servings a day.

To prepare a side dish (pictured, opposite) for the Mustard-Orange Pork Tenderloin, spray cut-up vegetables (such as red onions, carrots, zucchini, or yellow squash) with olive oil-flavored nonstick coating. Place them in the roasting pan around the roast. Roast them for 30 minutes or till tender.

TOTAL FAT: 6 g
DAILY VALUE FAT: 9%
DAILY VALUE SATURATED FAT: 10%

NUTRITION FACTS
PER SERVING:

Calories	257
Total Fat	6 g
Saturated Fat	2 g
Cholesterol	38 mg
Sodium	436 mg
Carbohydrate	33 g
Fiber	1 g
Protein	17 g

EXCHANGES:

1½ Starch, 2 Meat, 2 Vegetable

PREPARATION TIME: 50 minutes
COOKING TIME: 10 minutes

Ginger Pork Stir-Fry

Apple juice makes a subtle-sweet sauce for this tasty stir-fry. Always look for 100% pure juice when buying juices. Those labeled "drink" have more sugar than real juice.

12 ounces lean boneless pork
½ cup apple juice
3 tablespoons sodium-reduced soy sauce
1 tablespoon cornstarch
    Nonstick spray coating
2 teaspoons grated gingerroot
2 cups cauliflower flowerets
    (about ½ of a medium head)
1 medium zucchini, sliced
1 small onion, cut into thin wedges
2 cups hot cooked rice
    Red sweet pepper rings (optional)

● Trim any fat from pork. Partially freeze pork. Cut across the grain into thin bite-size strips.

● For sauce, in a small bowl stir together the apple juice, soy sauce, and cornstarch. Set aside.

● Spray a cold wok or large skillet with nonstick coating. Preheat over medium-high heat till a drop of water sizzles. Add gingerroot; stir-fry for 15 seconds. Add cauliflower; stir-fry for 2 minutes. Add zucchini and onion; stir-fry for 2 to 3 minutes more or till vegetables are crisp-tender. Remove vegetables from skillet.

● Add pork to skillet. Stir-fry about 3 minutes or till pork is no longer pink. Push pork from center of the wok or skillet. Stir sauce. Carefully add sauce to the center of the wok or skillet. Cook and stir till thickened and bubbly. Cook and stir for 1 minute more. Return vegetables to wok or skillet. Stir to coat with sauce. Heat through. Serve over hot rice. If desired, garnish with sweet red pepper rings. Makes 4 servings.

Pasta with Basil Cream Sauce

If you can't find prosciutto, substitute very thinly sliced lean ham.

6 **ounces linguine or fettuccine**
1 **cup shelled peas or frozen peas**
1 **12-ounce can (1⅓ cup) evaporated skim milk**
1 **tablespoon all-purpose flour**
1 **clove garlic, minced**
2 **tablespoons snipped basil**
2 **ounces prosciutto, chopped**
¼ **cup shredded Parmesan cheese**
2 **tablespoons shredded Parmesan cheese**
  Freshly ground black pepper
  Fresh basil leaves (optional)

● Cook pasta according to package directions except omit salt and oil.

● Meanwhile, cook fresh peas, if using, in a medium saucepan in a small amount of boiling water for 10 minutes. Drain; return to saucepan. Stir together the evaporated milk and flour. Add to cooked fresh peas in saucepan. Stir in garlic and snipped basil. Cook and stir over medium heat till mixture is thickened and bubbly. Cook and stir 1 minute more. (Add frozen peas, if using.) Add prosciutto and the ¼ cup Parmesan cheese. Stir till cheese is melted. *Do not boil.*

● To serve, pour sauce over cooked pasta. Toss to coat. Top with the 2 tablespoons Parmesan cheese and pepper. If desired, garnish with fresh basil. Makes 4 servings.

TOTAL FAT: 7 g
DAILY VALUE FAT: 11%
DAILY VALUE SATURATED FAT: 0%

NUTRITION FACTS PER SERVING:

Calories	353
Total Fat	7 g
Saturated Fat	0 g
Cholesterol	10 mg
Sodium	471 mg
Carbohydrate	50 g
Fiber	2 g
Protein	22 g

EXCHANGES:

1 Vegetable, 3 Starch, 2 Meat

PREPARATION TIME: 5 minutes
COOKING TIME: 15 minutes

Herb-Stuffed Pork Tenderloin

Tenderloins usually are packaged in 12- or 16-ounce portions, so you'll probably need to buy more than one. Freeze the extra and use it in a stir-fry for another meal.

18 ounces pork tenderloin
2 tablespoons Dijon-style mustard
1½ cups shredded romaine
½ cup assorted snipped herbs, such as sage, thyme, rosemary, dill, basil, marjoram, chervil, and/or savory
3 tablespoons fine dry bread crumbs
1 slightly beaten egg white
2 teaspoons olive oil or cooking oil
　Coarsely ground black pepper
　Snipped fresh chives (optional)
　Mustard Sauce

● Trim any fat from meat. Using a sharp knife, make a lengthwise cut down the center of roast, cutting to, but not through, the other side. Spread the meat flat. Place tenderloin between 2 sheets of plastic wrap and pound meat lightly with the flat side of a meat mallet to about a 13x8-inch rectangle. (If necessary, use a portion of a second tenderloin to make 18 ounces. Overlap and pound the pieces to make a single rectangle.) Fold in the narrow ends as necessary to make an even rectangle. Spread mustard evenly over tenderloin.

● Stir together romaine, herbs, bread crumbs, and egg white in a medium bowl. Spoon evenly over pork. Roll tenderloin up jelly-roll style, beginning at narrow end. Tie meat with string, first at center, then at 1-inch intervals.

● Place meat on rack in a shallow roasting pan. Brush oil over meat. Sprinkle with pepper. Roast, uncovered, in a 375° oven about 50 to 60 minutes or till meat is tender and slightly pink (160°) and juices run clear. Transfer to a warm platter. Remove strings; keep warm while preparing sauce. To serve, cut tenderloin into 12 slices. Spoon Mustard Sauce over each serving. Makes 6 servings.

Mustard Sauce: Combine ⅓ cup plain fat-free *yogurt*, 2 tablespoons fat-free *mayonnaise or salad dressing*, 1½ to 2 teaspoons *Dijon-style mustard*, and 1 teaspoon *honey* in a small saucepan. Cook over low heat for 2 to 3 minutes or just till heated through. *Do not boil.* Serve immediately with pork slices.

TOTAL FAT: 5 g
DAILY VALUE FAT: 8%
DAILY VALUE SATURATED FAT: 5%

NUTRITION FACTS PER SERVING:

Calories	162
Total Fat	5 g
Saturated Fat	1 g
Cholesterol	61 mg
Sodium	308 mg
Carbohydrate	6 g
Fiber	0 g
Protein	21 g

EXCHANGES:
3 Meat

PREPARATION TIME: 30 minutes
COOKING TIME: 50 minutes

TOTAL FAT: 8 g
DAILY VALUE FAT: 12%
DAILY VALUE SATURATED FAT: 10%

**NUTRITION FACTS
PER SERVING:**

Calories	172
Total Fat	8 g
Saturated Fat	2 g
Cholesterol	45 mg
Sodium	180 mg
Carbohydrate	1 g
Fiber	0 g
Protein	23 g

EXCHANGES:

3 Meat

PREPARATION TIME: 5 minutes
MARINATING TIME: 2 hours
COOKING TIME: 6 minutes

Rosemary-Marinated Swordfish

The small amount of oil in the marinade will keep the fish from drying out during cooking.

4   fresh or frozen swordfish, halibut, or
     tuna steaks, ¾-inch thick (1 pound
     total)
2   tablespoons white wine vinegar
1   tablespoon water
1   tablespoon olive oil or cooking oil
2   green onions, thinly sliced
2   teaspoons snipped fresh rosemary or
     ½ teaspoon dried rosemary, crushed
1   teaspoon white wine Worcestershire
     sauce
⅛   teaspoon salt
     Dash pepper
     Nonstick spray coating
     Fresh rosemary sprigs (optional)

● Thaw fish, if frozen. In a shallow dish combine vinegar, water, oil, onions, rosemary, Worcestershire sauce, salt, and pepper. Place the fish steaks in the marinade mixture, turning to coat. Cover and marinate in refrigerator for 2 hours, turning once.

● Drain fish, reserving marinade. Spray a cold grill rack with nonstick spray coating. Place fish on rack. Grill fish steaks on an uncovered grill directly over *medium-hot* coals for 4 minutes. Brush with marinade. Using a wide spatula turn the fish over. Grill for 2 to 5 minutes more or till fish begins to flake easily when tested with a fork. (To broil, spray the unheated rack of a broiler pan with nonstick spray coating. Place fish on rack. Broil 4 inches from the heat for 6 to 9 minutes or till fish just begins to flake easily when tested with a fork, brushing with marinade after 4 minutes.) If desired, garnish with fresh rosemary sprigs. Makes 4 servings.

Seafood Chowder

Choose firm-textured fish fillets, such as perch, cod, grouper, halibut, or orange roughy, for this chowder.

12 ounces fresh or frozen fish fillets
4 ounces fresh or frozen scallops
1½ cups water
2 small potatoes, peeled and cut into
  ½-inch cubes (1⅓ cups)
½ cup sliced green onion
½ cup shredded carrot (1 medium)
1½ teaspoons snipped fresh thyme or
  ½ teaspoon dried thyme, crushed
½ teaspoon instant chicken bouillon
  granules
1 12-ounce can (1½ cups) evaporated
  skim milk
2 tablespoons cornstarch
1 tablespoon snipped parsley (optional)

● Thaw fish and scallops, if frozen. Cut the fillets into 1-inch pieces. Halve any large scallops. In a medium saucepan stir together the water, potato, onion, carrot, thyme, and bouillon granules. Bring to boiling. Reduce heat. Simmer, covered, about 15 minutes or till the potatoes are nearly tender.

● Stir in fish and scallops. Return to boiling. Reduce heat. Simmer, covered, about 3 minutes or till fish nearly flakes when tested with a fork.

● In a small mixing bowl gradually stir milk into cornstarch. Stir into mixture in saucepan. Cook and stir over medium heat till thickened and bubbly. Cook and stir for 2 to 3 minutes more or till fish flakes easily when tested with a fork. To serve, ladle into serving bowls. If desired, sprinkle with parsley. Makes 4 servings.

Fish and Seafood Buying Guide

You don't have to be a fisherman to know a good fish when you see one. Here are a few tips to buying the freshest catch of the day:

Whole Fish. Look for eyes that are clear and bright, not sunken. The gills should be bright red or pink, the skin should be shiny and elastic, and the scales should be tight.

Fish Fillets and Steaks. Make sure the fish in the counter is displayed on a bed of ice. The fish should have a mild smell, not a strong, fishy odor. Avoid fish that is dry around the edges.

Shrimp. Pick fresh shrimp that are moist and firm, with translucent flesh and a fresh aroma. Avoid shrimp with an ammonia-like smell.

TOTAL FAT: 1 g
DAILY VALUE FAT: 2%
DAILY VALUE SATURATED FAT: 0%

NUTRITION FACTS PER SERVING:

Calories	217
Total Fat	1 g
Saturated Fat	0 g
Cholesterol	44 mg
Sodium	317 mg
Carbohydrate	26 g
Fiber	1 g
Protein	25 g

EXCHANGES:
½ Vegetable, 1½ Starch, 3 Meat

PREPARATION TIME: 15 minutes
COOKING TIME: 23 minutes

Salmon with Wilted Greens

This fish dinner packs in all the vitamin C and almost half of the vitamin A you need for an entire day — all for under 300 calories.

4 fresh or frozen salmon steaks,
    ¾-inch thick (1 pound total)
3 tablespoons orange juice concentrate
3 tablespoons water
2 tablespoons reduced-sodium soy sauce
1 tablespoon honey
2 teaspoons cooking oil
1 teaspoon toasted sesame oil
½ teaspoon grated gingerroot or
    ¼ teaspoon ground ginger
6 cups torn mixed greens, such as spinach,
    Swiss chard, radicchio, or mustard,
    beet, or collard greens
1 medium orange, peeled and sectioned
1 small red sweet pepper, cut into thin
    strips (½ cup)

● Thaw fish, if frozen. Set aside. For dressing, combine orange juice concentrate, water, soy sauce, honey, cooking oil, sesame oil, and gingerroot or ground ginger in a small bowl.

● Place salmon on the ungreased rack of a broiler pan. Broil 4 inches from heat for 5 minutes. Using a wide spatula, carefully turn salmon over. Brush with *1 tablespoon* of the dressing. Broil for 3 to 7 minutes more or till salmon just begins to flake easily when tested with a fork. (Or, to grill, place fish steaks on an ungreased grill rack. Grill fish on an uncovered grill directly over *medium-hot* coals for 5 minutes. Using a wide spatula, carefully turn fish over. Brush with *1 tablespoon* of the dressing. Grill for 3 to 7 minutes more or till fish flakes easily with a fork.) Cover and keep fish warm while preparing the greens.

● Place greens and orange sections in a large salad bowl. Bring remaining dressing mixture to boiling in a large skillet. Add red pepper strips. Remove from heat. Pour over greens, tossing to mix. To serve, divide greens among 4 dinner plates. Top each serving with a salmon steak. Serve immediately. Makes 4 servings.

TOTAL FAT: 9 g
DAILY VALUE FAT: 14%
DAILY VALUE SATURATED FAT: 10%

**NUTRITION FACTS
PER SERVING:**

Calories	255
Total Fat	9 g
Saturated Fat	2 g
Cholesterol	31 mg
Sodium	406 mg
Carbohydrate	15 g
Fiber	2 g
Protein	27 g

EXCHANGES:

2 Vegetable, ½ Fruit, 3 Meat

PREPARATION TIME: 10 minutes
COOKING TIME: 8 minutes

TOTAL FAT: **4 g**
DAILY VALUE FAT: **6%**
DAILY VALUE SATURATED FAT: **5%**

NUTRITION FACTS
PER SERVING:

Calories	116
Total Fat	4 g
Saturated Fat	1 g
Cholesterol	20 mg
Sodium	68 mg
Carbohydrate	3 g
Fiber	0 g
Protein	16 g

EXCHANGES:

2 Meat

PREPARATION TIME: **5 minutes**
COOKING TIME: **8 minutes**

Easy Citrus Salmon Steaks

Salmon contains omega-3 fatty acids, a type of polyunsaturated oil. This type of oil appears to help reduce blood pressure and the risk of heart disease and cancer.

> 2 **fresh or frozen salmon steaks, 1 inch thick (about 1 pound total)**
> 2 **teaspoons finely shredded lemon or orange peel**
> 2 **tablespoons lemon or orange juice**
> ¼ **teaspoon pepper**
> 2 **cloves garlic, minced**
> 2 **tablespoons sliced green onion**
> 1 **orange, peeled and thinly sliced crosswise**

● Thaw fish, if frozen. In a small mixing bowl stir together the lemon or orange peel, lemon or orange juice, pepper, and garlic.

● Spray an unheated rack of a broiler pan. Place salmon steaks on rack. Brush steaks with *half* of the lemon or orange juice mixture. Broil 4 to 5 inches from the heat for 5 minutes. Using a wide spatula, carefully turn salmon over. Broil for 3 to 7 minutes more or till fish flakes easily with a fork. To serve, cut the fish into 4 portions and sprinkle with green onion. Serve with orange slices. Makes 4 servings.

Hints for Cooking Fish

Just like any other meat, fish should not be undercooked or overcooked. Follow these visual guidelines in testing doneness:
● Properly cooked fish is opaque, with milky, white juices. The flesh flakes easily with a fork.
● Undercooked fish is translucent, with clear juices. The flesh is firm and does not flake easily.
● Overcooked fish is opaque and dry. The flesh flakes into little pieces when tested with a fork.

Mango-Shrimp Salad

Mangos bring 25 percent of your vitamins A and C for the day to a serving of this salad.

1 medium ripe mango
½ teaspoon finely shredded lime peel
3 tablespoons lime juice
1 tablespoon olive oil
1 tablespoon honey
½ of a fresh jalapeño pepper, seeded and chopped
12 ounces fresh or frozen shrimp
3 cups water
4 cups torn fresh spinach

● Peel mango. Cut flesh from seed (see tip below). Cut into ¾-inch pieces. In a blender container or food processor bowl combine *one-fourth* of the mango pieces, the lime peel, lime juice, olive oil, honey, and jalapeño pepper. Cover and blend or process till smooth. Cover and refrigerate for 1 to 4 hours. Cover and refrigerate remaining mango till needed.

● Thaw shrimp, if frozen. Peel and devein the shrimp. In a large saucepan bring water to boiling. Add the shrimp. Cover and simmer for 1 to 3 minutes or till shrimp turn pink; drain. Cover and refrigerate for 1 to 4 hours.

● For salad, halve chilled shrimp lengthwise. In a large mixing bowl combine the shrimp, chilled reserved mango, and spinach, tossing to mix. To serve, arrange salad mixture on 4 serving plates. Drizzle mango puree over each salad. Makes 4 servings.

Peeling a Mango

Removing the large seed in a mango takes a little cutting know-how. To begin, align a sharp knife slightly off-center of the stemmed end of the fruit. Slice through the peel and flesh, just next to the pit. Repeat on the other side. Cut off the flesh remaining around the seed. Remove the peel and cut the mango into pieces as directed.

TOTAL FAT: 4 g
DAILY VALUE FAT: 6%
DAILY VALUE SATURATED FAT: 5%

**NUTRITION FACTS
PER SERVING:**

Calories	162
Total Fat	4 g
Saturated Fat	1 g
Cholesterol	131 mg
Sodium	195 mg
Carbohydrate	16 g
Fiber	3 g
Protein	16 g

EXCHANGES:
1½ Vegetable, ½ Fruit, 2 Meat

PREPARATION TIME: 20 minutes
COOKING TIME: 1 minute
CHILLING TIME: 1 hour

Pasta with Fresh Tomato-Herb Sauce, recipe page 108

Vegetable Frittata, recipe page 121

Meatless Main Dishes

Choosing to go meatless a few times a week makes good sense when it comes to your health. Generally, meatless meals are lower in fat, saturated fat, and cholesterol. Limiting this three-some in your diet helps keep your heart strong and healthy. And that's easier to do when you have a collection of flavor-filled choices, such as Tortilla-Black Bean Casserole, Cream of Corn Chowder, Pasta with Red Pepper Sauce, or Lentil-Spinach Stew. Your heart and family will love you.

TOTAL FAT: 2 g
DAILY VALUE FAT: 3%
DAILY VALUE SATURATED FAT: 0%

NUTRITION FACTS
PER SERVING:

Calories	260
Total Fat	2 g
Saturated Fat	0 g
Cholesterol	0 mg
Sodium	15 mg
Carbohydrate	53 g
Fiber	2 g
Protein	9 g

EXCHANGES:
1½ Vegetable, 3 Starch

PREPARATION TIME: 38 minutes
STANDING TIME: 30 minutes
COOKING TIME: 25 minutes

Pasta with Fresh Tomato-Herb Sauce

Serve this dish for a light summer meal. Just add a small salad and a loaf of warm French bread. (See photograph on page 106 and cover.)

2 large tomatoes or 4 to 6 roma tomatoes, chopped (2 cups)
1 tablespoon snipped basil and/or oregano
2 cloves garlic, minced
¼ teaspoon pepper
6 ounces capellini, linguine, or spaghetti
2 tablespoon grated Parmesan cheese (optional)
Fresh basil (optional)

● In a medium mixing bowl gently toss together the tomatoes, desired herb, garlic, and pepper. Cover and let mixture stand at room temperature for 30 minutes to allow the flavors to blend. Meanwhile, cook pasta according to package directions, except omit any salt or oil; drain. Add the hot pasta to the tomato mixture. If desired, sprinkle with Parmesan cheese and garnish with fresh basil. Makes 3 servings.

The Truth About Pasta

If you avoid pasta because you think it's fattening, you're missing out on a nutritional bargain. Pasta is high in complex carbohydrates, which is important in a healthful eating plan. A cup of pasta, such as spaghetti or capellini, has about 150 calories and less than 1 gram of fat. So why does pasta have a high-fat reputation? Because of the sauces that often top it. Choose fresh, low-fat sauces like this one and make pasta a regular part of your meals.

Pasta with Red Pepper Sauce

This sweet pepper sauce is a pleasant change from tomato sauce. The peppers also shoots the sauce's vitamin C content sky-high, supplying more than three times the amount you need in one day.

6 medium red sweet peppers, chopped, or
    two 12-ounce jars roasted red sweet
    peppers, drained
4 cloves garlic, peeled
2 tablespoons olive oil
1 cup water
⅔ cup loosely packed fresh snipped basil
    or 2 tablespoons dried basil, crushed
½ cup tomato paste
2 tablespoons red wine vinegar
8 ounces pasta (penne, mostaccioli, or
    rigatoni), cooked and drained
    Shredded Parmesan cheese (optional)

● In a large skillet cook fresh red peppers, if using, and garlic in hot oil over medium heat about 20 minutes, stirring occasionally. (Or, if using peppers from a jar, which are already cooked, cook the garlic in hot oil for 3 to 4 minutes or till light brown.)

● Place *half* of the peppers and the garlic in a blender container or food processor bowl. Cover; blend or process till nearly smooth. Add *half* of the water, basil, tomato paste, and vinegar. Cover and blend or process with several on-off turns till basil is just chopped and mixture is nearly smooth. Transfer to a 2-quart saucepan. Repeat with remaining peppers, water, basil, tomato paste, and vinegar; transfer to saucepan.

● Cook and stir sauce over medium heat till heated through. Serve sauce over hot pasta with Parmesan cheese. Makes 4 servings.

TOTAL FAT: **8 g**
DAILY VALUE FAT: **12%**
DAILY VALUE SATURATED FAT: **5%**

**NUTRITION FACTS
PER SERVING:**

Calories	340
Total Fat	8 g
Saturated Fat	1 g
Cholesterol	0 mg
Sodium	28 mg
Carbohydrate	60 g
Fiber	2 g
Protein	10 g

EXCHANGES:
3 Starch, 2 Vegetable, 1½ Fat

**PREPARATION TIME: 15 minutes
COOKING TIME: 25 minutes**

TOTAL FAT: 3 g
DAILY VALUE FAT: 5%
DAILY VALUE SATURATED FAT: 0%

NUTRITION FACTS
PER SERVING:

Calories	319
Total Fat	3 g
Saturated Fat	0 g
Cholesterol	0 mg
Sodium	116 mg
Carbohydrate	62 g
Fiber	5 g
Protein	12 g

EXCHANGES:
3 Vegetable, 3 Starch, ½ Fat

PREPARATION TIME: 10 minutes
COOKING TIME: 25 minutes

Fettuccine with Vegetable Sauce

For this tomato-based pasta sauce, you may choose any frozen vegetable combination your family likes.

2 cloves garlic, minced
¾ cup chopped onion
1 teaspoon olive oil or cooking oil
1 14½-ounce can low-sodium tomatoes, cut up
1 8-ounce can low-sodium tomato sauce
2 teaspoons Italian seasoning, crushed
1 teaspoon fennel seed, crushed
¼ teaspoon pepper
⅛ teaspoon salt
2 cups loose-pack frozen broccoli, red pepper, mushroom, and onion
8 ounces spinach or plain fettuccine, linguine, or spaghetti
Freshly shredded Parmesan cheese (optional)

● For sauce, in a large saucepan cook garlic and onion in hot oil till tender. Stir in *undrained* tomatoes, tomato sauce, Italian seasoning, fennel seed, pepper, and salt. Bring to boiling. Reduce heat. Simmer, uncovered, for 15 minutes, stirring occasionally. Stir in frozen vegetables. Return to boiling. Reduce heat. Simmer, uncovered, for 4 to 5 minutes more or till vegetables are tender, stirring occasionally.

● Meanwhile, cook pasta according to package directions, except omit any oil or salt. Drain. Serve sauce over hot cooked pasta. If desired, sprinkle with Parmesan cheese. Makes 4 servings.

Fresh vs. Frozen Fruits and Vegetables

Q. Is fresh produce more nutritious than frozen or canned produce?

A. Not necessarily. Here's why:.

● Unless it's homegrown or grown locally, produce may not reach your market for several days. During that long trip, it may lose flavor, moisture, and nutrients.

● Commercially harvested produce usually is frozen or canned within 4 to 6 hours of harvesting, when nutrient content is high. Some nutrients are lost during processing, but the shorter the time between harvest and processing, the better the nutrients are retained.

Sometimes convenience dictates using frozen or canned produce in certain dishes. Generally, though, when deciding which form to use, buy what suits your family's needs best.

Deli-Style Pasta Salad

In a hurry? Substitute bottled nonfat Italian salad dressing for the homemade dressing.

TOTAL FAT: **12 g**
DAILY VALUE FAT: **18%**
DAILY VALUE SATURATED FAT: **10%**

NUTRITION FACTS
PER SERVING:

Calories	305
Total Fat	12 g
Saturated Fat	2 g
Cholesterol	30 mg
Sodium	315 mg
Carbohydrate	41 g
Fiber	4 g
Protein	13 g

EXCHANGES:

2 Vegetable, ½ Meat, 2 Bread, 2 Fat

PREPARATION TIME: **15 minutes**
CHILLING TIME: **1 hour**
COOKING TIME: **8 minutes**

½ **of a 16-ounce package frozen or one 9-ounce package refrigerated cheese-filled tortellini (about 2 cups)**
1½ **cups broccoli flowerets**
¾ **cup thinly sliced carrot (1 large)**
¾ **cup chopped red or yellow sweet pepper (1 medium)**
¼ **cup white wine vinegar**
2 **tablespoons olive oil**
1 **teaspoon Italian seasoning, crushed**
1 **teaspoon Dijon-style mustard**
¼ **teaspoon pepper**
⅛ **teaspoon garlic powder**
  Kale leaves (optional)

● In a large saucepan cook pasta according to package directions, except omit salt and oil. Add the broccoli, carrot, and red or yellow sweet pepper to the pasta during the last 3 minutes of cooking time. Return to boiling. Reduce heat. Simmer, uncovered, for 3 minutes or till pasta is al dente and vegetables are crisp-tender. Drain. Rinse with cold water. Drain.

● For dressing, in a screw-top jar combine the vinegar, olive oil, Italian seasoning, mustard, pepper, and garlic powder. Cover and shake to combine. Pour over pasta mixture; toss to coat. Cover and chill for 1 to 2 hours. Stir mixture before serving. If desired, serve atop kale leaves. Makes 4 servings.

TOTAL FAT: **7 g**
DAILY VALUE FAT: **11%**
DAILY VALUE SATURATED FAT: **5%**

NUTRITION FACTS
PER SERVING:

Calories	274
Total Fat	7 g
Saturated Fat	1 g
Cholesterol	0 mg
Sodium	161 mg
Carbohydrate	44 g
Fiber	7 g
Protein	12 g

EXCHANGES:

1 Vegetable, 2½ Starch, ½ Meat,
1 Fat

PREPARATION TIME: **22 minutes**
CHILLING TIME: **4 hours**

Tabbouleh and Bean Salad

Traditional tabbouleh (tuh-BOO-luh), a middle Eastern salad, generally contains mint. This version contains fresh basil. Spoon it into a pita bread round, if you like, for a great sandwich.

¾ cup bulgur
1 15½-ounce can reduced-sodium dark red
    kidney beans or one 15-ounce can
    black beans, rinsed and drained
1 cup chopped, seeded cucumber
    (½ of a medium)
½ cup sliced green onion
¼ cup snipped parsley
2 cloves garlic, minced
¼ cup lemon juice
2 tablespoons olive oil
1 tablespoon snipped fresh basil or
    1 teaspoon dried basil, crushed
¼ teaspoon salt
¼ teaspoon pepper
    Lettuce leaves (optional)
1 large tomato, chopped

● In a colander rinse the bulgur with cold water. Drain. In a medium mixing bowl stir together the bulgur, drained beans, cucumber, green onion, and parsley.

● For dressing, in a screw-top jar combine the garlic, lemon juice, olive oil, basil, salt, and pepper. Cover; shake to mix. Pour over bulgur mixture. Toss to coat. Cover and chill for 4 to 24 hours. If desired, line 4 serving plates with lettuce leaves. Stir the tomato into the tabbouleh mixture. Spoon atop lettuce leaves. Makes 4 servings.

The Benefits of Bulgur

Bulgur wheat is made from wheat kernels that have been steamed, dried, and crushed into small pieces. A half-cup serving has 114 calories, less than ½ gram of fat, and is a good source of carbohydrates and protein. You'll find bulgur next to the rice in your supermarket. It's available in a variety of grain sizes; choose the finer-crushed bulgur for tabbouleh.

Creamy Lentil Salad

This salad is hearty enough for a main dish. Like pasta, the lentils should be cooked till they are al dente, *or slightly firm to the bite.*

¾ cup dry lentils
1½ cups water
½ teaspoon instant chicken or vegetable
    bouillon granules
½ cup chopped green sweet pepper
⅓ cup shredded carrot
½ cup low-calorie creamy cucumber salad
    dressing
½ teaspoon dried dillweed
4 cups purchased torn mixed salad greens
1 cup cherry tomatoes, halved
2 tablespoons sliced almonds, toasted

● Rinse lentils. Drain. In a medium saucepan combine lentils, water, and bouillon granules. Bring to boiling. Reduce heat. Simmer, covered, about 20 minutes or till liquid is absorbed and lentils are tender. Stir in green pepper and carrot. Cover and chill for 1 to 2 hours.

● To serve, stir the salad dressing and dillweed into the lentil mixture. In a medium mixing bowl toss together salad greens and tomatoes. Arrange tomato mixture on 4 serving plates. Top each salad with lentil mixture. Sprinkle with almonds. Makes 4 servings.

Love Those Lentils

Lentils are eaten in many parts of the world as a meat substitute, as they are a good source of protein. Additionally, they supply fiber, calcium, vitamin B, iron, and phosphorus to your diet. With a bean-like texture and a mild, nutty flavor, they're an excellent addition to salads, casseroles, soups, and stews.

TOTAL FAT: 6 g
DAILY VALUE FAT: 9%
DAILY VALUE SATURATED FAT: 0%

NUTRITION FACTS
PER SERVING:

Calories	218
Total Fat	6 g
Saturated Fat	0 g
Cholesterol	0 mg
Sodium	564 mg
Carbohydrate	29 g
Fiber	3 g
Protein	12 g

EXCHANGES:

2 Vegetable, 1 Starch, 1 Meat,
½ Fat

PREPARATION TIME: 10 minutes
CHILLING TIME: 1 hours
COOKING TIME: 20 minutes

Tortilla-Black Bean Casserole

Using low-fat dairy products makes this family favorite more healthful. Low-fat sour cream, salsa, and sliced green onions are tasty toppers, too.

TOTAL FAT: 4 g
DAILY VALUE FAT: 6%
DAILY VALUE SATURATED FAT: 5%

NUTRITION FACTS
PER SERVING:

Calories	248
Total Fat	4 g
Saturated Fat	1 g
Cholesterol	0 mg
Sodium	631 mg
Carbohydrate	40 g
Fiber	5 g
Protein	15 g

EXCHANGES:

2 Vegetable, 3 Starch, 2 Meat,
½ Fat

PREPARATION TIME: 20 minutes
COOKING TIME: 35 minutes

2 cups chopped onion
1½ cups chopped green sweet pepper
1 14½-ounce can tomatoes, cut up
¾ cup picante sauce
2 cloves garlic, minced
2 teaspoons ground cumin
2 15-ounce cans black beans or red kidney
    beans, drained and rinsed
    Nonstick spray coating
10 7-inch corn tortillas
2 cups shredded reduced-fat Monterey
    Jack cheese (8 ounces)
    Shredded lettuce (optional)
    Sliced small fresh red chili peppers
    (optional)

● In a large skillet combine the onion, green pepper, *undrained* tomatoes, picante sauce, garlic, and cumin. Bring to boiling; reduce heat. Simmer, uncovered, for 10 minutes. Stir in the beans.

● Spray a 2-quart-rectangular baking dish with nonstick coating. Spread *one-third* of the bean mixture over bottom of the dish. Top with *half* of the tortillas, overlapping as necessary, and *half* of the cheese. Add another *one-third* of the bean mixture, then remaining tortillas and bean mixture. Cover and bake in a 350° oven for 35 to 40 minutes or till heated through. Sprinkle with remaining cheese. Let stand for 10 minutes.

● If desired, place some shredded lettuce on each serving plate. To serve, cut casserole into squares; place atop lettuce. Garnish with chili peppers, if desired. Makes 6 to 8 servings.

Lentil-Spinach Stew

A mere half cup of cooked lentils has 9 grams of protein, 4 grams of fiber, and zero fat. How's that for nutritious?

TOTAL FAT: 4 g
DAILY VALUE FAT: 6%
DAILY VALUE SATURATED FAT: 5%

NUTRITION FACTS
PER SERVING:

Calories	248
Total Fat	4 g
Saturated Fat	1 g
Cholesterol	0 mg
Sodium	631 mg
Carbohydrate	40 g
Fiber	5 g
Protein	15 g

EXCHANGES:

2 Vegetable, 2 Starch, 1 Meat

PREPARATION TIME: 15 minutes
COOKING TIME: 40 minutes

1 cup dry lentils
2 cloves garlic, minced
1 medium onion, chopped (½ cup)
1 tablespoon cooking oil
4 cups water
1 7½-ounce can tomatoes, cut up
2 teaspoons instant vegetable or chicken bouillon granules
1 tablespoon Worcestershire sauce
½ teaspoon dried thyme, crushed
¼ teaspoon fennel seed, crushed
¼ teaspoon pepper
1 bay leaf
2 medium carrots, chopped (1 cup)
1 10-ounce package frozen chopped spinach
1 tablespoon balsamic vinegar or red wine vinegar

● Rinse lentils; set aside. In a large saucepan or Dutch oven cook the garlic and onion in hot oil till tender but not brown. Stir in the lentils, water, *undrained* tomatoes, bouillon granules, Worcestershire sauce, thyme, fennel seed, pepper, and bay leaf. Bring to a boil; reduce heat. Cover and simmer for 20 minutes.

● Add carrots and frozen spinach. Bring to a boil, breaking up spinach with a fork; reduce heat. Cover and simmer about 15 minutes more or till lentils are tender. Stir in vinegar. Discard bay leaf. Makes 4 servings.

TOTAL FAT: 2 g
DAILY VALUE FAT: 3%
DAILY VALUE SATURATED FAT: 0%

NUTRITION FACTS
PER SERVING:

Calories	217
Total Fat	2 g
Saturated Fat	0 g
Cholesterol	2 mg
Sodium	505 mg
Carbohydrate	45 g
Fiber	1 g
Protein	10 g

EXCHANGES:

1 Milk, 2 Starch, ½ Fat

PREPARATION TIME: 15 minutes
COOKING TIME: 20 minutes

Cream of Corn Chowder

Bright red sweet pepper and yellow corn make this soup as colorful as confetti. Serve it as a main dish for three or a side dish for four.

1   14½-ounce can reduced-sodium chicken broth
1   10-ounce package frozen whole kernel corn
2   cloves garlic, minced
1   small potato, peeled and cubed (about ⅔ cup)
1   medium onion, chopped (½ cup)
1   small red or green sweet pepper, chopped (½ cup)
¼   cup water
½   teaspoon dried marjoram or thyme, crushed
¼   teaspoon ground cumin
    Dash salt
½   of a 12-ounce can (¾ cup) evaporated skim milk
4   teaspoons cornstarch

● In a medium saucepan combine chicken broth, corn, garlic, potato, onion, red or green sweet pepper, water, marjoram or thyme, cumin, and salt. Bring to boiling. Reduce heat. Simmer, covered, for 15 to 20 minutes or till vegetables are tender.

● Gradually stir milk into cornstarch. Stir into mixture in saucepan. Cook and stir over medium heat till thickened and bubbly. Cook and stir for 2 minutes more. Makes 3 servings.

Vegetable Frittata

When you need a spur-of-the-moment meal, this egg dish saves the day. Serve it with sliced fresh tomatoes or cucumbers topped with a light vinaigrette and a hearty bread. (See photograph on pages 106 and 107.)

1 cup water
1 cup broccoli flowerets
½ cup finely chopped carrot
¼ cup sliced green onion
   Nonstick spray coating
¾ cup shredded reduced-fat cheddar or
   Swiss cheese (3 ounces)
2 8-ounce cartons refrigerated or frozen
   egg product, thawed
1 tablespoon snipped fresh basil or
   1 teaspoon dried basil, crushed
1 tablespoon Dijon-style mustard
¼ teaspoon pepper
   Tomato slices (optional)
   Fresh tarragon (optional)

● In a medium saucepan combine water, broccoli, and carrot. Bring to boiling. Reduce heat. Simmer, covered, for 6 to 8 minutes or till vegetables are crisp-tender. Drain well.

● Spray a large nonstick skillet with nonstick coating. Spread cooked broccoli, carrot, and green onion in the bottom of skillet. Sprinkle *half* the cheese over vegetables. In a medium mixing bowl stir together egg product, basil, mustard, and pepper. Pour over vegetables and cheese in skillet. Cook over medium heat. As mixture sets, run a spatula around edge of skillet, lifting egg mixture to allow uncooked portions to flow underneath. Continue cooking and lifting the edges till egg mixture is almost set (the surface will be moist).

● Remove skillet from heat. Cover and let stand for 3 to 4 minutes or till top is set. To serve, cut into wedges. Sprinkle with remaining cheese. If desired, garnish with tomato slices and tarragon. Makes 8 servings.

TOTAL FAT: 3 g
DAILY VALUE FAT: 5%
DAILY VALUE SATURATED FAT: 5%

NUTRITION FACTS
PER SERVING:

Calories	101
Total Fat	3 g
Saturated Fat	1 g
Cholesterol	6 mg
Sodium	287 mg
Carbohydrate	6 g
Fiber	0 g
Protein	11 g

EXCHANGES:
1 Vegetable, 1½ Meat

PREPARATION TIME: 18 minutes
COOKING TIME: 8 minutes

TOTAL FAT: **8 g**
DAILY VALUE FAT: **12%**
DAILY VALUE SATURATED FAT: **10%**

NUTRITION FACTS
PER SERVING:

Calories	230
Total Fat	8 g
Saturated Fat	2 g
Cholesterol	11 mg
Sodium	460 mg
Carbohydrate	23 g
Fiber	0 g
Protein	15 g

EXCHANGES:

1½ Starch, 1½ Meat, ½ Fat

PREPARATION TIME: **15 minutes**
COOKING TIME: **13 minutes**

Mexican-Style Scrambled Eggs

Extra-sharp cheddar cheese is more flavorful than its milder cousins—you don't have to use as much, which means fewer calories and less fat.

 1 cup water
¼ cup thinly sliced green onion
¼ cup chopped red or green sweet pepper
 1 8-ounce carton refrigerated or frozen egg product, thawed
¼ cup skim milk
⅛ teaspoon pepper
 4 7-inch flour tortillas, warmed
 1 teaspoon margarine or butter
½ cup shredded reduced-fat cheddar cheese (2 ounces)
⅓ cup salsa

● In a small saucepan combine water, onion, and sweet pepper. Bring to boiling. Reduce heat. Simmer, uncovered, for 5 to 7 minutes or till the vegetables are tender. Drain well. In a medium mixing bowl stir together egg product, milk, and pepper. Stir in drained vegetables.

● To warm tortillas, wrap tortillas in aluminum foil; bake in a 350° oven for 15 minutes. Remove from oven, but leave tortillas in closed foil packet to keep warm.

● Meanwhile, in a large skillet melt margarine or butter over medium heat. Pour in egg-product mixture. Cook, without stirring, till mixture begins to set on the bottom and around the edges. Using a large spoon or spatula, lift and fold partially cooked eggs so uncooked portion flows underneath. Sprinkle with cheese. Continue cooking for 2 to 3 minutes or till eggs are cooked throughout but are still glossy and moist. (Be careful not to overcook the egg mixture.) Remove from heat immediately.

● To serve, spoon the egg mixture down the center of warm tortillas. Fold each tortilla in half or roll up. Top with the salsa. Makes 4 servings.

Spinach Quiche

If you use frozen spinach, micro-cook it on 100% power (high) for 45 to 60 seconds. Then use a large knife to cut the partially-thawed block in half and return the unused portion to your freezer.

Baked Pastry Shell
- **8 cups torn fresh spinach or ½ of a 10-ounce package frozen chopped spinach, thawed**
- **½ cup water**
- **½ cup chopped onion**
- **½ cup chopped red sweet pepper**
- **2 cloves garlic, minced**
- **1 tablespoon snipped fresh basil or ¾ teaspoon dried basil, crushed**
- **¼ teaspoon salt**
- **1 8-ounce carton refrigerated or frozen egg product, thawed**
- **1 cup evaporated skim milk**
- **1 tablespoon all-purpose flour**
- **1 tablespoon grated Parmesan cheese Several dashes bottled hot pepper sauce**

● Prepare Baked Pastry Shell. Reduce oven temperature to 350°. Meanwhile, in a medium saucepan combine spinach, water, onion, red pepper, and garlic. Bring to boiling. Reduce heat. Simmer, uncovered, for 2 to 3 minutes or till spinach and onion are tender. Drain well, pressing out excess moisture with the back of a spoon. Stir in basil and salt.

● Spoon spinach mixture into pastry shell. In a medium mixing bowl stir together egg product, milk, flour, Parmesan cheese, and hot pepper sauce. Pour over spinach mixture. Bake in a 350° oven for 40 to 45 minutes or till a knife inserted near the center comes out clean. Let stand for 10 minutes before serving. Makes 8 servings.

Baked Pastry Shell: In a medium mixing bowl stir together 1¼ cups *all-purpose flour* and ⅛ teaspoon *salt*. Using a pastry blender, cut in ¼ cup *shortening* till pieces are the size of small peas. Sprinkle 1 tablespoon *water* over *half* of the mixture; gently toss with a fork. Push moistened dough to the side of the bowl. Moisten the remaining dough, using 1 tablespoon of water at a time, till all dough is moistened. Form dough into a ball. On a lightly floured surface, slightly flatten dough. Roll dough from center to edges, to form a circle about 12 inches in diameter. Ease pastry into a 9-inch pie plate, being careful not to stretch pastry. Trim pastry to ½ inch beyond edge of pie plate. Fold under extra pastry; flute edge. Do not prick pastry. Line pastry with a double thickness of foil. Bake in a 450° oven for 8 minutes. Remove foil. Bake for 4 to 5 minutes more or till set and dry.

TOTAL FAT: **8 g**
DAILY VALUE FAT: **12%**
DAILY VALUE SATURATED FAT: **10%**

NUTRITION FACTS
PER SERVING:

Calories	**199**
Total Fat	**8 g**
Saturated Fat	**2 g**
Cholesterol	**2 mg**
Sodium	**214 mg**
Carbohydrate	**22 g**
Fiber	**2 g**
Protein	**10 g**

EXCHANGES:

1 Vegetable, 1 Starch, 1 Meat, 1 Fat

PREPARATION TIME: **35 minutes**
COOKING TIME: **40 minutes**
STANDING TIME: **10 minutes**

Cheesy Polenta Squares, recipe page 126

Grilled Herbed Vegetables,
recipe page 127

Side Dishes

What would chicken be without potatoes and gravy, or turkey without stuffing? Side dishes help make the meal. Here you'll find healthful ways to add spark and sizzle to an otherwise ordinary meal. Side dishes add color to your plate and, most importantly, lots of nutrients. Serve Wild Rice with Walnuts and Dates, Oriental Potato and Chick Pea Salad, or Lemony Asparagus and New Potatoes with a simple cut of meat and transform a so-so meal into a source of pleasure and praise.

TOTAL FAT: **2 g**
DAILY VALUE FAT: **3%**
DAILY VALUE SATURATED FAT: **5%**

**NUTRITION FACTS
PER SERVING:**

Calories	89
Total Fat	2 g
Saturated Fat	1 g
Cholesterol	5 mg
Sodium	206 mg
Carbohydrate	13 g
Fiber	1 g
Protein	5 g

EXCHANGES:

1 Starch, ½ Fat

PREPARATION TIME: 20 minutes
STANDING TIME: 30 minutes
COOKING TIME: 10 minutes

Cheesy Polenta Squares

Polenta, an Italian favorite, is made from cornmeal. For a spicy flavor, top it with warm spaghetti or pizza sauce (See photograph on page 124.)

    Nonstick spray coating
1½ **cups skim milk**
½ **cup cornmeal**
½ **cup cold water**
¼ **teaspoon salt**
¼ **cup plain low-fat yogurt**
¼ **cup grated Parmesan cheese**
    Dash ground red pepper
    **Spaghetti or pizza sauce, heated
    (optional)**

● Spray an 8x8x2-inch baking pan with nonstick spray coating. In a 2-quart saucepan heat milk to simmering.

● Meanwhile, in a mixing bowl stir together cornmeal, cold water, and salt. Gradually add cornmeal mixture to simmering milk, stirring constantly. Cook and stir till mixture returns to simmering; reduce heat. Cook, uncovered, over low heat about 10 minutes or till thick, stirring frequently. Spread cornmeal mixture in prepared pan. Let stand, uncovered, for 30 to 40 minutes or till mixture is firm.

● Meanwhile, in a small bowl combine the yogurt, Parmesan cheese, and ground red pepper. Set mixture aside.

● Spray an oval baking dish or 15x10x1-inch baking pan with nonstick coating. Transfer polenta to prepared pan or dish. Spoon the yogurt mixture over the polenta.

● Bake, uncovered, in a 425° oven for 10 to 12 minutes or till top is golden and polenta is heated through. If desired, serve with warm spaghetti or pizza sauce. Makes 6 servings.

Grilled Herbed Vegetables

For easy cleanup and fuss-free cooking, bake or grill mixed veggies of your choice in a foil packet.
(See photograph on pages 124 and 125.)

1 tablespoon olive oil
1 clove garlic, minced
2 teaspoon snipped fresh rosemary or
    ½ teaspoon dried rosemary, crushed; or
    2 tablespoon snipped fresh basil or
    1 teaspoon dried basil, crushed
¼ teaspoon salt
4 cups mixed vegetables, such as eggplant
    chunks; halved small yellow squash,
    zucchini, or pattypan squash; green
    beans; red onion wedges; and/or sliced
    yellow, red, or green sweet pepper
Pepper

In a medium mixing bowl combine the olive oil, garlic, rosemary or basil, and the salt. Let mixture stand for 2 hours.

Add the vegetables to oil mixture, tossing to coat. Spoon vegetable mixture onto a 24x12-inch piece of heavy foil. Bring opposite edges of foil together; seal tightly with a double fold. Fold in remaining ends to completely enclose vegetables, leaving a little space for steam to build.

Grill the vegetable packet on a grill rack directly over *medium-hot* coals about 20 minutes or till vegetables are tender, turning the packet over halfway through the cooking time. (Or, bake vegetables in a 350° oven about 25 minutes or till tender.) Season vegetables to taste with pepper. Makes 4 servings.

Eat Your Vegetables

Our moms were right. We *should* eat our vegetables, because they provide our bodies with vitamins A and C, folic acid, iron, magnesium, and other important nutrients. In addition, they're low in fat and tops in fiber. But can we really eat 3 to 5 servings of them every day? Absolutely. It's easy to meet your minimum goal for the day when you consider that the following equals one serving:

- 1 cup of raw leafy vegetables, such as spinach, cabbage, or lettuce
- ½ cup of chopped vegetables, cooked or raw, such as carrots, potatoes, or corn
- ¾ cup of vegetable juice

TOTAL FAT: **4 g**
DAILY VALUE FAT: **6%**
DAILY VALUE SATURATED FAT: **0%**

NUTRITION FACTS PER SERVING:

Calories	63
Total Fat	4 g
Saturated Fat	0 g
Cholesterol	0 mg
Sodium	136 mg
Carbohydrate	8 g
Fiber	3 g
Protein	1 g

EXCHANGES:
1 Vegetable, 1 Fat

PREPARATION TIME: 5 minutes
STANDING TIME: 2 hours
COOKING TIME: 20 minutes

Jicama Coleslaw

Store whole jicamas in the refrigerator for up to 3 weeks. If cut up, wrap them in plastic wrap and refrigerate for up to 1 week.

2 cups shredded cabbage
1 cup julienne, peeled jicama
1 medium apple, chopped, or 1 medium peach or nectarine, peeled, pitted, and chopped
½ of a small red onion, chopped (about ¼ cup)
3 tablespoons reduced-calorie mayonnaise dressing or salad dressing
2 tablespoons snipped cilantro or parsley
1 tablespoon cider vinegar
1½ teaspoons sugar
Dash to ⅛ teaspoon ground red pepper
Purple kale (optional)

● In a large mixing bowl combine cabbage; jicama; apple, peach or nectarine; and red onion.

● In a small bowl stir together mayonnaise or salad dressing, cilantro or parsley, vinegar, sugar, and ground red pepper. Pour dressing over cabbage mixture, tossing to combine. Cover and chill for 2 to 4 hours. Place in a salad bowl. If desired, garnish with kale. Makes 4 servings.

Have Some Jicama

Jicama (pronounced *HE kuh muh*) actually resembles a large, brown turnip. The thin, pale brown skin peels off easily to reveal a pure white, potato-like meat that has a clean, crisp bite and a mildly sweet flavor. It is best when peeled just before using and can be eaten raw or cooked.

TOTAL FAT: 4 g
DAILY VALUE FAT: 6%
DAILY VALUE SATURATED FAT: 5%

NUTRITION FACTS PER SERVING:

Calories	91
Total Fat	4 g
Saturated Fat	1 g
Cholesterol	0 mg
Sodium	91 mg
Carbohydrate	14 g
Fiber	2 g
Protein	1 g

EXCHANGES:
1 Vegetable, ½ Fruit, 1 Fat

PREPARATION TIME: 20 minutes
CHILLING TIME: 2 hours

TOTAL FAT: **5 g**
DAILY VALUE FAT: **8%**
DAILY VALUE SATURATED FAT: **10%**

NUTRITION FACTS
PER SERVING:

Calories	134
Total Fat	5 g
Saturated Fat	2 g
Cholesterol	5 mg
Sodium	171 mg
Carbohydrate	22 g
Fiber	3 g
Protein	4 g

EXCHANGES:
1½ Starch, 1 Fat

PREPARATION TIME: **10 minutes**
COOKING TIME: **5 minutes**

Spiced Corn Raita

Raita is a traditional Indian salad that combines yogurt with fresh vegetables. In this dish, toasting the cumin and mustard seeds brings out their unique flavors. The serrano pepper lends a bit of heat.

> 2 cups cooked fresh or frozen whole kernel corn, drained and cooled
> ½ cup plain low-fat or fat-free yogurt
> 2 tablespoons fat-free dairy sour cream
> ¼ teaspoon salt
> 1½ teaspoons cooking oil
> ¼ teaspoon cumin seed
> ¼ teaspoon mustard seed
> 1 fresh serrano pepper, seeded and finely chopped
> Leaf lettuce (optional)
> Chopped red or green sweet pepper (optional)

● In a medium mixing bowl combine cooled corn, yogurt, sour cream, and salt. In a small saucepan combine oil, cumin seed, mustard seed, and serrano pepper. Place over low heat and cook about 5 minutes or just till mustard seeds begin to "dance." (Do not overheat or seeds will pop out of the pan.)

● Stir the mustard seed mixture into the corn mixture. Serve immediately or cover and chill for up to 4 hours. To serve, if desired, line a serving dish with lettuce leaves; top with corn mixture. Sprinkle with chopped red or green pepper. Makes 4 servings.

Sizzlin' Serrano

Don't let the small size of a serrano pepper fool you. It may be tiny, but it packs a spicy punch. Usually dark green in color, serranos sometimes are allowed to ripen to a red color. They're also available canned and pickled. In this dish you may substitute a jalapeño pepper, which ranges from hot to sizzling.

Orange-Glazed Brussels Sprouts and Carrots

One serving of this vegetable dynamo meets all your vitamin C needs for the day.

2 cups brussels sprouts or one 10-ounce package frozen brussels sprouts, thawed

3 medium carrots, cut lengthwise into quarters, then into 1-inch pieces

⅓ cup orange juice

1 teaspoon cornstarch

½ teaspoon sugar

¼ teaspoon salt

¼ teaspoon ground nutmeg (optional)

● Cut brussels sprouts in half. In a medium saucepan combine sprouts and carrots. Cook, covered, in a small amount of boiling water for 10 to 12 minutes or till crisp-tender. Drain well. Return all of the vegetables to pan.

● In a bowl combine the orange juice, cornstarch, sugar, salt, and nutmeg, if desired. Add to brussels sprouts and carrots. Cook and stir the mixture over medium heat till thickened and bubbly. Cook and stir for 1 minute more. [Or, to microwave, halve the brussels sprouts as directed. In a 1½-quart microwave-safe casserole, micro-cook fresh brussels sprouts, carrots, and 2 tablespoons *water,* covered, on 100% power (high) for 6 to 8 minutes or till crisp-tender, stirring once. Drain. In a small bowl stir together the orange juice, cornstarch, sugar, salt, and nutmeg, if desired. Add to brussels sprouts and carrots. Micro-cook, uncovered, on high for 2 to 3 minutes or till mixture is bubbly, stirring every 30 seconds.] Serve immediately. Makes 4 servings.

TOTAL FAT: 1 g
DAILY VALUE FAT: 2%
DAILY VALUE SATURATED FAT: 0%

NUTRITION FACTS PER SERVING:

Calories	67
Total Fat	1 g
Saturated Fat	0 g
Cholesterol	0 mg
Sodium	184 mg
Carbohydrate	15 g
Fiber	5 g
Protein	3 g

EXCHANGES:
1 Vegetable, ½ Fruit

PREPARATION TIME: 10 minutes
COOKING TIME: 12 minutes

TOTAL FAT: 3 g
DAILY VALUE FAT: 5%
DAILY VALUE SATURATED FAT: 0%

NUTRITION FACTS
PER SERVING:

Calories	105
Total Fat	3 g
Saturated Fat	0 g
Cholesterol	0 mg
Sodium	141 mg
Carbohydrate	19 g
Fiber	2 g
Protein	3 g

EXCHANGES:

1 Starch, ½ Vegetable, ½ Fat

PREPARATION TIME: 10 minutes
COOKING TIME: 18 minutes

Lemony Asparagus and New Potatoes

With spring comes fresh asparagus and new potatoes. This recipe showcases both in a healthful side dish with a snippet of lemon and thyme.

12 ounce asparagus spears
 8 whole tiny new potatoes, cut into
      quarters (about 10 ounces)
 2 teaspoons olive oil or cooking oil
 ½ teaspoon finely shredded lemon peel
 ¼ teaspoon salt
 ¼ teaspoon dried thyme, crushed
      Fresh thyme (optional)

● Snap off and discard woody bases from asparagus. If desired, scrape off scales. Cut into 2-inch pieces. Set aside.

● In a 2-quart saucepan cook potatoes, covered, in a small amount of boiling water for 10 minutes. Add asparagus. Cook, covered, about 8 minutes more or till asparagus is crisp-tender and potatoes are tender; drain. Transfer vegetables to a serving bowl.

● Meanwhile, for dressing, in a small bowl combine the olive oil, shredded lemon peel, salt, and thyme. Add to the vegetables, tossing gently to coat. Garnish with fresh thyme, if desired. Serve warm. Makes 4 servings.

TOTAL FAT: 6 g

DAILY VALUE FAT: 9%

DAILY VALUE SATURATED FAT: 5%

NUTRITION FACTS PER SERVING:

Calories	197
Total Fat	6 g
Saturated Fat	1 g
Cholesterol	0 mg
Sodium	300 mg
Carbohydrate	32 g
Fiber	3 g
Protein	7 g

EXCHANGES:

2 Starch, 1 Fat

PREPARATION TIME: 5 minutes

COOKING TIME: 60 minutes

Wild Rice with Walnuts and Dates

Sweet dates make all the difference in this delicious side dish. The dates and walnuts also add fiber.

4 stalks celery, chopped (2 cups)
1 small onion, chopped (¼ cup)
1 tablespoon margarine or butter
1 cup wild rice, rinsed and drained
1 14½-ounce chicken, beef, or vegetable broth
1 cup water
⅓ cup pitted whole dates, snipped
¼ cup chopped walnuts, toasted

● In a 10-inch skillet cook celery and onion in hot margarine or butter about 10 minutes or till tender. Add *uncooked* wild rice; cook and stir for 3 minutes. Add the broth and water. Bring to boiling; reduce heat. Simmer, covered, for 50 to 60 minutes or till most of the liquid is absorbed and rice is tender.

● Stir in the dates and walnuts. Cook, uncovered, for 3 to 4 minutes more or till heated through and the remaining liquid is absorbed. Makes 6 to 8 servings.

The Perfect Date

To add fiber to your diet, depend on all-natural dates. Just 3 medium dates have as much fiber as 2 cups of puffed wheat cereal! Toss them into pancake batter, muffins, cereal, or vanilla yogurt—they'll add a candy-like sweetness with more nutrition than you'll find in a chocolate chip.

Oriental Potato and Chick Pea Salad

This salad supplies almost one-fourth of your fiber and almost half of your vitamin C needs for the day.

¾ **cup frozen loose-pack cut green beans**
1 **16-ounce can sliced white potatoes, drained and rinsed**
1¼ **cups chick peas (garbanzo beans), rinsed and drained (¾ of a 15-ounce can)**
1 **small red or green sweet pepper, chopped (⅔ cup)**
2 **tablespoons sliced green onion**
¼ **cup white wine vinegar**
1 **tablespoon honey mustard**
1 **tablespoon reduced-sodium soy sauce**
1 **teaspoon sesame seed, toasted**
1 **teaspoon toasted sesame oil**
⅛ **teaspoon pepper**

● In a small saucepan cook the green beans according to package directions; drain. Combine cooked green beans, potatoes, chick peas, sweet pepper, and green onion in a large bowl.

● For dressing, in a small bowl stir together the vinegar, honey mustard, soy sauce, sesame seed, sesame oil, and pepper. Add to potato mixture, gently tossing to coat. Cover and chill at least 2 hours. Makes 4 servings.

TOTAL FAT: 3 g
DAILY VALUE FAT: 5%
DAILY VALUE SATURATED FAT: 0%

NUTRITION FACTS PER SERVING:

Calories	160
Total Fat	3 g
Saturated Fat	0 g
Cholesterol	0 mg
Sodium	664 mg
Carbohydrate	30 g
Fiber	6 g
Protein	6 g

EXCHANGES:
2 Starch, ½ Fat

PREPARATION TIME: 5 minutes
COOKING TIME: 10 minutes
CHILLING TIME: 2 hours

Watermelon Sherbet, recipe page 138

Cinnamon Meringues with Fruit,
recipe page 139

Desserts

Saving the best for last certainly pertains to desserts, but for many of us, that last little offering of sweets causes more than a little concern. With this repertoire of treasures, however, we've taken out the worry and kept in the pleasure for you. Imagine being able truly to enjoy Pecan Ice-Cream Roll, Mini Cheesecakes, Oranges in Caramel Sauce, or Summer Fruit Tart. You'll be proud to serve them and delighted to eat them—without the usual pangs of guilt.

TOTAL FAT: **0 g**
DAILY VALUE FAT: **0%**
DAILY VALUE SATURATED FAT: **0%**

NUTRITION FACTS
PER SERVING:

Calories	**83**
Total Fat	**0 g**
Saturated Fat	**0 g**
Cholesterol	**0 mg**
Sodium	**3 mg**
Carbohydrate	**20 g**
Fiber	**0 g**
Protein	**1 g**

EXCHANGES:

1½ Fruit

PREPARATION TIME: **25 minutes**
FREEZING TIME: **8 hours**

Watermelon Sherbet

This refreshing after-dinner treat is a welcome change from fat-laden ice creams. (See photograph on page 136.)

4 cups cubed, seeded watermelon
½ cup sugar
1 envelope unflavored gelatin
⅓ cup cranberry juice cocktail

● Place watermelon cubes in a blender container or food processor bowl. Cover and blend or process till smooth. (There should be 3 cups of the mixture.) Stir in sugar.

● In a small saucepan combine gelatin and cranberry juice cocktail. Let mixture stand for 5 minutes. Stir mixture over low heat till gelatin is dissolved.

● Stir the gelatin mixture into the melon mixture. Pour into an 8x8x2-inch baking pan. Cover and freeze about 2 hours or till firm.

● Break up frozen mixture and place in a chilled mixer bowl. Beat with an electric mixer on medium to high speed or till mixture is fluffy. Return to pan. Cover and freeze about 6 hours or till firm. Makes 8 (½-cup) servings.

Selecting the Perfect Melon

You've probably thumped a few melons to check for ripeness. You need thump no more. Instead, pick a perfect melon according to color. A ripe watermelon should have an even, dull, and pale to dark green color with a creamy yellow underside. Avoid choosing those with soft ends. When buying pre-cut melons, look for those with firm, brightly-colored, juicy-looking flesh.

Cinnamon Meringues with Fruit

You may either pipe the meringues from a pastry bag or simply spoon them onto the baking sheet. For crispy meringue shells, serve them right away. However, if you like softer, marshmallow-like shells, chill them for up to 2 hours before serving. (See photograph on page 136 and 137.)

2 egg whites
½ teaspoon vanilla
½ teaspoon ground cinnamon
¼ teaspoon cream of tartar
½ cup sugar
2 cups sliced, peeled peaches or nectarines
2 tablespoons sugar
1 tablespoon cornstarch
2 cups fresh fruit, such as sliced peeled peaches, nectarines, or kiwi fruit; and/or sliced strawberries

● For meringue shells, cover a baking sheet with plain brown paper.* Draw six 3x3-inch squares or six 3½-inch diameter circles on the paper. In a small mixing bowl beat the egg whites, vanilla, cinnamon, and cream of tartar with an electric mixer on medium speed till soft peaks form. Gradually add the ½ cup sugar, beating on high speed till stiff peaks form and sugar is almost dissolved.

● Spoon meringue mixture into a decorating bag fitted with a medium plain-round or star tip (about ¼-inch opening). Pipe shells onto the prepared baking sheet. (Or, using a spoon or a spatula, spread meringue mixture over the square or circle on the prepared baking sheet, building the sides up to form a shell.)

● Bake in a 300° oven for 30 minutes. Turn off the heat and let shells dry in the oven with the door closed at least 1 hour more. *(Do not open oven.)* Peel off paper.

● For the sauce, place the 2 cups peaches or nectarines in a blender container or food processor bowl. Cover and blend or process till nearly smooth. Pour into a small saucepan. Combine the 2 tablespoons sugar and the cornstarch; add to saucepan. Cook and stir over medium heat till thickened and bubbly. Cook and stir for 2 minutes more.

● To serve, place a meringue shell on each of 6 dessert plates. Spoon sauce into shells. Top with fresh fruit. Serve immediately or cover and chill for up to 2 hours. Makes 6 servings.

Note: Use only paper that is specially made for baking purposes. Brown paper bags may contain materials that can catch fire in the oven and also may not be very sanitary.

TOTAL FAT: 0 g
DAILY VALUE FAT: 0%
DAILY VALUE SATURATED FAT: 0%

NUTRITION FACTS PER SERVING:

Calories	138
Total Fat	0 g
Saturated Fat	0 g
Cholesterol	0 mg
Sodium	19 mg
Carbohydrate	34 g
Fiber	3 g
Protein	2 g

EXCHANGES:

1 Starch, 1 Fruit

PREPARATION TIME: 25 minutes
COOKING TIME: 30 minutes
STANDING TIME: 1 hour

TOTAL FAT: 1 g
DAILY VALUE FAT: 2%
DAILY VALUE SATURATED FAT: 0%

**NUTRITION FACTS
PER SERVING:**

Calories	116
Total Fat	1 g
Saturated Fat	0 g
Cholesterol	0 mg
Sodium	5 mg
Carbohydrate	29 g
Fiber	2 g
Protein	1 g

EXCHANGES:
1½ Fruit

PREPARATION TIME: 15 minutes
COOKING TIME: 30 minutes

Chocolate-Sauced Pears

Go ahead—splurge. These luscious pears contain less than 120 calories and only 1 gram of fat per serving.

4 **small pears**
2 **tablespoons lemon juice**
2 **teaspoons vanilla**
½ **teaspoon ground cinnamon**
2 **tablespoons chocolate-flavored syrup**

● Core pears from bottom end, leaving stems intact. Peel pears. If necessary, cut a thin slice from bottoms of pears to help stand upright.

● Place pears in a 2-quart-square baking dish. Stir together lemon juice, vanilla, and cinnamon. Brush onto pears. Pour any extra lemon juice mixture over pears.

● Bake, covered, in a 375° oven for 30 to 35 minutes or till pears are tender. Cool slightly.

● To serve, place warm pears, stem end up, on dessert plates. Strain baking liquid; pour liquid into a small bowl. Stir in chocolate-flavored syrup. Drizzle sauce over pears. Serve warm. Makes 4 servings.

TOTAL FAT: **3 g**
DAILY VALUE FAT: **5%**
DAILY VALUE SATURATED FAT: **0%**

**NUTRITION FACTS
PER SERVING:**

Calories	95
Total Fat	3 g
Saturated Fat	2 g
Cholesterol	8 mg
Sodium	85 mg
Carbohydrate	17 g
Fiber	2 g
Protein	3 g

EXCHANGES:
1 Fruit, ½ Fat

PREPARATION TIME: 10 minutes

Peach Cups with Lemon Cream

Some of the best things in life aren't fussy. In-season peaches and berries make this dessert delicious. The lemon cream tastes ultra-rich, but uses up only 5 percent of your total fat limit for the day.

2 **large peaches or nectarines, halved and pitted**
½ **cup fresh or frozen red raspberries, thawed**
½ **cup fresh or frozen blueberries, thawed**
  Lemon Cream

● Place a peach or nectarine half, cut side up, in each of 4 serving dishes. Top each with raspberries and blueberries. Spoon Lemon Cream over each. Makes 4 servings.

Lemon Cream: Combine one-fourth of an 8-ounce container reduced-fat *cream cheese product,* softened; 2 tablespoons low-fat *lemon yogurt;* 1 tablespoon *honey;* and dash *ground ginger* in a small bowl. Beat with an electric mixer till smooth. Use immediately or cover and chill till serving time. Store in refrigerator for up to 1 week. Makes ¾ cup.

Having Your Just Desserts

Health experts recommend eating more fruits and vegetables that are rich in beta carotene, vitamin C, and fiber. The dessert, above, supplies all three—plus it's low in fat and saturated fat, proving that sweets *can* be part of a healthful diet.

Summer Fruit Tart

The pastry for this tart contains less fat and saturated fat than most other pastries made with shortening. Use it whenever you make single-crust pies.

Flaky Tart Shell
¼ cup **sugar**
2 tablespoons **cornstarch**
1 12-ounce can (1½ cups) **evaporated skim milk**
¼ cup **refrigerated or frozen egg product, thawed**
½ teaspoon **vanilla**
2 medium **peaches or nectarines, peeled, pitted, and thinly sliced**
2 **plums, pitted and thinly sliced**
2 **kiwi fruit, peeled and sliced**
¼ cup **blueberries or blackberries**
2 tablespoons **honey**
1 tablespoon **rum or orange juice**

● Prepare Flaky Tart Shell.

● For the filling, in a heavy medium saucepan stir together the sugar and cornstarch; stir in evaporated milk and egg product. Cook and stir the mixture over medium heat till mixture is thickened and bubbly. Cook and stir for 2 minutes more. Remove saucepan from heat. Stir in the vanilla. Cover the surface of filling with plastic wrap; chill thoroughly.

● Spread cooled filling into the baked tart shell. Arrange peaches or nectarines, plums, and kiwi fruit in concentric circles atop filling. Add berries to the center and randomly sprinkle any extra berries over the top.

● In a small bowl combine the honey and rum or orange juice. Brush honey mixture over fruit. Cover and chill for up to 1 hour. Before serving, remove sides of pan. Makes 10 servings.

Flaky Tart Shell: In a medium mixing bowl stir together 1¼ cups *all-purpose flour* and ¼ teaspoon *salt*. In a 1-cup measure combine ¼ cup *skim milk* and 3 tablespoons *cooking oil*. Add oil mixture all at once to flour mixture. With a fork stir together till dough forms. Shape dough into a ball. On a slightly floured surface, flatten the ball of dough with hands. Roll dough from center to the edges, forming a circle about 13 inches in diameter. Ease pastry into a 11-inch tart pan with a removable bottom, being careful not to stretch the pastry. Trim the pastry even with the edge of the pan. Prick pastry generously with the tines of a fork. Bake in a 450° oven for 10 to 12 minutes or till pastry is golden. Cool on a wire rack.

TOTAL FAT: 5 g
DAILY VALUE FAT: 8%
DAILY VALUE SATURATED FAT: 0%

NUTRITION FACTS PER SERVING:

Calories	194
Total Fat	5 g
Saturated Fat	1 g
Cholesterol	1 mg
Sodium	108 mg
Carbohydrate	32 g
Fiber	1 g
Protein	6 g

EXCHANGES:
1 Fruit, 1 Starch, 1 Fat

PREPARATION TIME: 15 minutes
CHILLING TIME: 1 hours
COOKING TIME: 10 minutes

TOTAL FAT: **4 g**
DAILY VALUE FAT: **6%**
DAILY VALUE SATURATED FAT: **0%**

NUTRITION FACTS
PER CHEESECAKE:

Calories	124
Total Fat	4 g
Saturated Fat	1 g
Cholesterol	5 mg
Sodium	25 mg
Carbohydrate	16 g
Fiber	0 g
Protein	6 g

EXCHANGES:
½ Milk, ½ Starch, 1 Fat

PREPARATION TIME: **20 minutes**
COOKING TIME: **18 minutes**
CHILLING TIME: **4 hours**

Mini Cheesecakes

Top these tiny cheesecakes with whatever fruit strikes your fancy. The small size makes perfect party treats or light desserts.

   Nonstick spray coating
⅓ **cup crushed vanilla wafers (8 wafers)**
1½ **8-ounce tubs fat-free cream cheese, softened (12 ounces total)**
½ **cup sugar**
1 **tablespoon all-purpose flour**
1 **teaspoon vanilla**
¼ **cup frozen egg product, thawed**
¾ **cup red raspberries; blueberries; sliced, peeled kiwi fruit; sliced strawberries; sliced, pitted plums; and/or orange sections**

● Spray 10 muffin cups with nonstick coating. Sprinkle bottom and sides of each cup with about *1 teaspoon* of the crushed vanilla wafers. Set pan aside.

● In a medium mixing bowl beat cream cheese with an electric mixer on medium speed till smooth. Add sugar, flour, and vanilla. Beat on medium speed till smooth. Add egg product and beat on low speed just till combined. Divide evenly among the muffin cups.

● Bake in a 325° oven for 18 to 20 minutes or till set. Cool in pan on a wire rack for 5 minutes. Cover and chill for 4 to 24 hours. Remove cheesecakes from the muffin cups. Just before serving, top cheesecakes with fresh fruit. Makes 10 cheesecakes.

TOTAL FAT: 0 g
DAILY VALUE FAT: 0%
DAILY VALUE SATURATED FAT: 0%

NUTRITION FACTS
PER SERVING:

Calories	106
Total Fat	0 g
Saturated Fat	0 g
Cholesterol	0 mg
Sodium	2 mg
Carbohydrate	25 g
Fiber	1 g
Protein	1 g

EXCHANGES:
1½ Fruit

PREPARATION TIME: 30 minutes
CHILLING TIME: 2 hours

Oranges in Caramel Sauce

Homemade caramel sauce turns fruit into an elegant, light dessert. With just over 100 calories and not a speck of fat, it will be a welcomed dessert. Try the sauce over poached pears or apples, too.

½ **cup sugar**
1 **cup warm water**
2 **tablespoons light rum or**
    ¼ **teaspoon rum flavoring**
6 **medium oranges**
    Fresh red raspberries (optional)
    Fresh mint leaves (optional)

● For sauce, in a heavy small skillet place sugar. Heat over medium-high heat till sugar begins to melt, shaking skillet occasionally to heat sugar evenly. *Do not stir.* Reduce heat to low; cook about 5 minutes more or till sugar is melted and golden. Stir as necessary after sugar begins to melt and as mixture bubbles. Remove from heat.

● Slowly and carefully pour in the warm water. Return to heat and cook on low heat till caramel dissolves. Slowly stir in rum or rum flavoring. Bring to boiling; reduce heat. Simmer mixture for 5 minutes; cool.

● Using a vegetable peeler, remove the peel (orange part only) from 1 orange. Cut peel into very thin strips and add to sugar mixture. Using a sharp small knife, remove the white membrane from all of the oranges.

● Slice oranges crosswise and place in a shallow dish. Pour caramel sauce over oranges. Cover and chill at least 2 hours or overnight.

● To serve, divide orange slices among 6 dessert dishes. Spoon the caramel sauce over each serving. If desired, garnish with fresh raspberries and mint leaves. Makes 6 servings.

Mocha Custards

Healthful eating doesn't mean you have to forego dessert. Just choose something light, like this mocha treat.

2¼ cups skim milk
⅓ cup sugar
2 tablespoons unsweetened cocoa powder
1 teaspoon instant coffee crystals
¾ cup refrigerated or frozen egg product, thawed
1 teaspoon vanilla
Fresh red raspberries (optional)

● In a medium saucepan combine the milk, sugar, cocoa powder, and coffee crystals. Cook and stir just till cocoa and coffee are dissolved.

● In a medium mixing bowl gradually add hot milk mixture to egg product. Stir in vanilla. Place six 6-ounce custard cups in a 3-quart-rectangular baking dish. Pour egg mixture into the custard cups. Place on the oven rack. Carefully, pour *boiling water* around the custard cups into the baking dish to a depth of about 1 inch.

● Bake in a 325° oven for 30 to 35 minutes or till a knife inserted near the center comes out clean. Remove the cups from the pan. Cool to room temperature. Chill in the refrigerator about 2 hours or till firm. Using a knife, loosen edges of custards, slipping the point of the knife down the sides. Invert custards onto dessert plates. If desired, garnish with fresh raspberries. Makes 6 servings.

TOTAL FAT: 1 g
DAILY VALUE FAT: 2%
DAILY VALUE SATURATED FAT: 0%

NUTRITION FACTS
PER SERVING:

Calories	112
Total Fat	1 g
Saturated Fat	0 g
Cholesterol	2 mg
Sodium	103 mg
Carbohydrate	17 g
Fiber	0 g
Protein	7 g

EXCHANGES:
1 Starch, 1 Meat

PREPARATION TIME: 15 minutes
COOKING TIME: 30 minutes
CHILLING TIME: 2 hours

Brownie-Fruit Pizza

To make the brownie crust easier to cut, spray a pizza cutter or knife with nonstick spray coating.

½ cup sugar
3 tablespoons margarine or butter, softened
¼ cup refrigerated or frozen egg product, thawed
¾ cup chocolate-flavored syrup
⅔ cup all-purpose flour
3 cups fresh fruit, such as sliced, peeled, and quartered kiwi fruit; sliced, peeled peaches; sliced nectarines or strawberries; red raspberries or blueberries
½ cup chocolate-flavored syrup

● Spray a 12-inch pizza pan with nonstick coating. Set aside.

● For crust, in a medium mixer bowl combine sugar and margarine. Beat with an electric mixer on medium speed till creamy. Add egg product; beat well. Alternately add the ¾ cup chocolate-flavored syrup and the flour, beating after each addition on low speed till combined. Spread into the prepared pizza pan.

● Bake in a 350° oven about 20 minutes or till top springs back when lightly touched. Cool in pan on a wire rack.

● To serve, cut brownie into 12 wedges. Top each wedge with fruit. Drizzle with remaining chocolate-flavored syrup. Makes 12 servings.

TOTAL FAT: 4 g
DAILY VALUE FAT: 6%
DAILY VALUE SATURATED FAT: 0%

NUTRITION FACTS PER SERVING:

Calories	169
Total Fat	4 g
Saturated Fat	1 g
Cholesterol	0 mg
Sodium	60 mg
Carbohydrate	35 g
Fiber	1 g
Protein	2 g

EXCHANGES:

1 Fruit, 1 Starch, 1 Fat

PREPARATION TIME: 15 minutes
COOKING TIME: 20 minutes

TOTAL FAT: **2 g**
DAILY VALUE FAT: **3%**
DAILY VALUE
SATURATED FAT: **0%**

NUTRITION FACTS
PER SERVING:

Calories	104
Total Fat	2 g
Saturated Fat	0 g
Cholesterol	1 mg
Sodium	152 mg
Carbohydrate	19 g
Fiber	1 g
Protein	3 g

EXCHANGES:

½ Fruit, ½ Starch, ½ Fat

PREPARATION TIME: **12 minutes**

Berry-Lemon Trifle

This simple dessert starts with angel food cake. Either a homemade or a bakery cake will do.

2 cups cubed angel food cake
1 8-ounce carton lemon fat-free yogurt
¼ of an 8-ounce container frozen light
   whipped dessert topping, thawed
1 cup mixed berries, such as red
   raspberries, blueberries, or sliced
   strawberries
Fresh mint (optional)

● Divide the angel food cake cubes among 4 dessert dishes. In a small mixing bowl fold together the yogurt and whipped topping. Dollop yogurt mixture atop cake cubes. Sprinkle with berries. If desired, garnish with fresh mint. Makes 4 servings.

Food of the Angels

How did angel food cake earn such a heavenly name? Maybe it's because a slice (1/12 of a cake) has about 130 calories and less than 1 gram of fat. A similar serving of homemade chocolate cake has over 300 calories and 13 grams of fat. When you want to splurge, angel food cake is definitely more saintly.

TOTAL FAT: 8 g
DAILY VALUE FAT: 12%
DAILY VALUE SATURATED FAT: 0%

NUTRITION FACTS
PER SERVING:

Calories	271
Total Fat	8 g
Saturated Fat	2 g
Cholesterol	18 mg
Sodium	439 mg
Carbohydrate	47 g
Fiber	1 g
Protein	4 g

EXCHANGES:

1 Fruit, 2 Starch, 1½ Fat

PREPARATION TIME: 25 minutes
COOKING TIME: 35 minutes

Orange-Chocolate Cake

Some chocolate cakes with heavy frosting can have as much as 30 grams of fat per serving! The drizzle of frosting on this citrus-flavored cake is just as satisfying and more healthful.

    Unsweetened cocoa powder
1 package 2-layer-size devil's food
      cake mix
1 8-ounce carton plain fat-free or low-fat
      yogurt
2 tablespoons finely shredded orange peel
½ cup orange juice
½ cup water
1 egg
2 egg whites
2 tablespoons cooking oil
1 teaspoon ground cinnamon
    Chocolate Icing
    Orange Icing

● Spray a 10-inch fluted tube pan or a 13x9x2-inch baking pan with nonstick coating; dust with unsweetened cocoa powder. Set aside.

● In a large mixer bowl combine the cake mix, yogurt, orange peel, orange juice, water, whole egg, egg whites, cooking oil, and cinnamon. Beat with an electric mixer on low speed for 4 minutes. Pour into prepared pan.

● Bake in a 350° oven for 40 to 50 minutes for fluted tube pan or 35 to 40 minutes for the 13x9x2-inch baking pan or till a toothpick inserted near center comes out clean. Cool cake in pan about 10 minutes. Remove cake from tube pan, if using. Cool the cake completely on a wire rack. Drizzle icings over cake. Makes 12 servings.

Chocolate Icing: In a small bowl combine ½ cup sifted *powdered sugar*, 1 tablespoon *unsweetened cocoa powder*, 2 teaspoons *orange juice*, and ¼ teaspoon *vanilla*. Stir in additional *orange juice* till of drizzling consistency.

Orange Icing: In another small bowl combine ½ cup *sifted powdered sugar*, 1 teaspoon *orange juice*, and ¼ teaspoon *vanilla*. Stir in additional *orange juice* till of drizzling consistency.

Pineapple Ice

You don't need an ice-cream freezer to make this intensely flavored ice—simply put it in a freezer container and freeze overnight.

1 **20-ounce can crushed pineapple (juice pack)**
½ **cup sugar**
2 **cups buttermilk or one 16-ounce carton plain fat-free yogurt**
½ **teaspoon vanilla**
    Fresh pineapple (optional)
    Mint leaves (optional)

● In a blender container or food processor bowl place the *undrained* pineapple. Cover and blend or process till pureed. Transfer the pureed pineapple to a mixing bowl; stir in sugar. Let the mixture stand about 10 minutes or till the sugar dissolves, stirring occasionally. Stir in the buttermilk or yogurt and vanilla.

● Transfer pineapple mixture to a 1½-quart freezer container. Cover and freeze overnight or till firm. Let stand at room temperature about 30 minutes before serving. Scoop into small dessert bowls. If desired, garnish with fresh pineapple or mint leaves. Makes 8 to 9 servings.

No-Butter Buttermilk

Buttermilk's name may fool you, but its nutritional advantages won't. As you can see, it's even lower in calories, fat, and saturated fat than an 8-ounce serving of 1% milk. Made from nonfat or low-fat milk, buttermilk gets its tang from the addition of friendly bacteria.

	Calories	Fat (grams)	Saturated Fat (grams)
Buttermilk	99	2.2	1.3
1% skim milk	102	2.6	1.6
Whole milk (3.3% fat)	150	8.2	5.1

TOTAL FAT: 1 g
DAILY VALUE FAT: 2%
DAILY VALUE SATURATED FAT: 0%

NUTRITION FACTS PER SERVING:

Calories	117
Total Fat	1 g
Saturated Fat	0 g
Cholesterol	2 mg
Sodium	66 mg
Carbohydrate	27 g
Fiber	0 g
Protein	2 g

EXCHANGES:
1½ Fruit, ½ Starch

PREPARATION TIME: 20 minutes
FREEZING TIME: 12 hours

Pecan Ice-Cream Roll

Make this elegant, splurge dessert up to 2 weeks in advance and store it, tightly wrapped, in your freezer.

⅓ **cup all-purpose flour**
¼ **cup unsweetened cocoa powder**
1 **teaspoon baking powder**
¼ **teaspoon salt**
4 **egg yolks**
½ **teaspoon vanilla**
⅓ **cup granulated sugar**
4 **egg whites**
½ **cup granulated sugar**
   Sifted powdered sugar
1 **quart fat-free vanilla ice cream, softened**
¼ **cup broken pecans**
   Raspberry Sauce (optional)
   Fresh raspberries (optional)
   Fresh mint sprigs (optional)

● Grease and flour a 15x10x1-inch jelly-roll pan. Stir together flour, cocoa powder, baking powder, and salt. Set aside.

● In a small mixing bowl beat egg yolks and vanilla with an electric mixer on high speed about 5 minutes or till thick and lemon-colored. Gradually add the ⅓ cup sugar, beating on medium speed about 5 minutes or till sugar is almost dissolved. Thoroughly wash beaters.

● In a large mixing bowl beat egg whites on medium to high speed till soft peaks form (tips curl). Gradually add the ½ cup granulated sugar, beating till stiff peaks form (tips stand straight). Fold yolk mixture into the egg white mixture. Sprinkle flour mixture over egg mixture; fold in gently, just till combined. Spread batter evenly into prepared pan.

● Bake in 375° oven for 12 to 15 minutes or till the top springs back when lightly touched. Immediately loosen edges of cake from pan; turn out onto a clean dish towel sprinkled with sifted powdered sugar. Starting with a narrow end, roll up cake and towel together. Cool on a wire rack.

● Unroll the cake. Spread softened ice cream onto cake to within 1 inch of edges. Sprinkle with pecans. Reroll cake without towel. Wrap and freeze at least 4 hours before serving. To serve, if desired, drizzle Raspberry Sauce over the serving plates. Slice the cake; place on plates. If desired, garnish with raspberries and mint. Makes 10 servings.

Raspberry Sauce: In a small saucepan combine ⅔ cup *seedless raspberry spreadable fruit,* 1 tablespoon *lemon juice,* and ¼ teaspoon *almond extract.* Cook and stir just till melted. Cool slightly.

TOTAL FAT: **5 g**
DAILY VALUE FAT: **8%**
DAILY VALUE SATURATED FAT: **5%**

NUTRITION FACTS
PER SERVING:

Calories	211
Total Fat	5 g
Saturated Fat	1 g
Cholesterol	85 mg
Sodium	171 mg
Carbohydrate	38 g
Fiber	0 g
Protein	6 g

EXCHANGES:

2½ Starch, 1 Fat

PREPARATION TIME: **45 minutes**
BAKING TIME: **12 minutes**
COOLING TIME: **30 minutes**
FREEZING TIME: **4 hours**

Keep track of your daily nutrition needs by using the information we provide with each recipe. We've analyzed the nutritional content of each recipe serving for you. When a recipe gives an ingredient substitution, we used the first choice in the analysis. If it makes a range of servings (such as 4 to 6), we used the smallest number. Ingredients listed as optional weren't included in the calculations.

Metric Cooking Hints

By making a few conversions, cooks in Australia, Canada, and the United Kingdom can use the recipes in Better Homes and Gardens® *Low-fat & Luscious* with confidence. The charts on this page provide a guide for converting measurements from the U.S. customary system, which is used throughout this book, to the imperial and metric systems. There also is a conversion table for oven temperatures to accommodate the differences in oven calibrations.

Volume and Weight: Americans traditionally use cup measures for liquid and solid ingredients. The chart (top right) shows the approximate imperial and metric equivalents. If you are accustomed to weighing solid ingredients, here are some helpful approximate equivalents.
● 1 cup butter, caster sugar, or rice = 8 ounces = about 250 grams
● 1 cup flour = 4 ounces = about 125 grams
● 1 cup icing sugar = 5 ounces = about 150 grams

Spoon measures are used for smaller amounts of ingredients. Although the size of the tablespoon varies slightly among countries, for practical purposes and for recipes in this book, a straight substitution is all that's necessary.

Measurements made using cups or spoons should always be level, unless stated otherwise.

Product Differences: Most of the ingredients called for in the recipes in this book are available in English-speaking countries. However, some are known by different names. Here are some common American ingredients and the possible counterparts:
● Sugar is granulated or caster sugar.
● Powdered sugar is icing sugar.
● All-purpose flour is plain household flour or white flour. When self-rising flour is used in place of all-purpose flour in a recipe that calls for leavening, omit the leavening agent (baking soda or baking powder) and salt.
● Light corn syrup is golden syrup.
● Cornstarch is cornflour.
● Baking soda is bicarbonate of soda.
● Vanilla is vanilla essence.

Useful Equivalents

⅛ teaspoon = 0.5 ml
¼ teaspoon = 1 ml
½ teaspoon = 2 ml
1 teaspoon = 5 ml
¼ cup = 2 fluid ounces = 50 ml
⅓ cup = 3 fluid ounces = 75 ml
½ cup = 4 fluid ounces = 125 ml

⅔ cup = 5 fluid ounces = 150 ml
¾ cup = 6 fluid ounces = 175 ml
1 cup = 8 fluid ounces = 250 ml
2 cups = 1 pint
2 pints = 1 litre
½ inch = 1 centimetre
1 inch = 2 centimetres

Baking Pan Sizes

American	Metric
8x1½-inch round baking pan	20x4-centimetre sandwich or cake tin
9x1½-inch round baking pan	23x3.5-centimetre sandwich or cake tin
11x7x1½-inch baking pan	28x18x4-centimetre baking pan
13x9x2-inch baking pan	32.5x23x5-centimetre baking pan
2-quart-rectangular baking dish	30x19x5-centimetre baking pan
15x10x2-inch baking pan	38x25.5x2.5-centimetre baking pan (Swiss roll tin)
9-inch pie plate	22x4- or 23x4-centimetre pie plate
7- or 8-inch springform pan	18- or 20-centimetre springform or loose-bottom cake tin
9x5x3-inch loaf pan narrow loaf pan or paté tin	23x13x6-centimetre or 2-pound
1½-quart casserole	1.5-litre casserole
2-quart casserole	2-litre casserole

Oven Temperature Equivalents

Fahrenheit Setting	Celsius Setting*	Gas
300°F	150°C	Gas Mark 2
325°F	160°C	Gas Mark 3
350°F	180°C	Gas Mark 4
375°F	190°C	Gas Mark 5
400°F	200°C	Gas Mark 6
425°F	220°C	Gas Mark 7
450°F	230°C	Gas Mark 8
Broil		Grill

*Electric and gas ovens may be calibrated using Celsius. However, increase the Celsius setting 10 to 20 degrees when cooking above 160°C with an electric oven. For convection or forced-air ovens (gas or electric), lower the temperature setting 10°C when cooking at all heat levels.